BLOOM'S ReViews

COMPREHENSIVE RESEARCH & STUDY GUIDES

Charlotte Brontë's

Jane Eyre

Edited & with
an Introduction
by Harold Bloom

1

3 5 7 9 8 6 4 2

ISBN: 0-7910-4132-8

Chelsea House Publishers
1974 Sproul Road, Suite 400
P.O. Box 914
Broomall, PA 19008-0914

The Chelsea House World Wide Web address is
www.chelseahouse.com

Contents

Editor's Note

My Introduction traces the analogues between Jane Eyre's relation to Rochester, and Charlotte Brontë's relations to Lord Byron and to males among her reading audience.

Critical extracts begin with some early reviews: Henry F. Chorley praises the novel's realistic intensity, but E. P. Whipple oddly finds "blasphemy and ribaldry" in *Jane Eyre*. Lady Eastlake goes further in denouncing Charlotte Brontë for supposed anti-Christian stances, but the poet Swinburne exalts her for her powers of characterization. Leslie Stephen commends Brontë for individuality, and Augustine Birrell for her sheer vitality. Rather differently, Leslie Stephen's daughter, the novelist Virginia Woolf, reads *Jane Eyre* as a visionary poem.

The contest between Jane and Rochester is analyzed by Richard Chase, while Robert B. Heilman sees the book as transfigured Gothic. Cosmological scope is found by R. B. Martin to be the principal strength of the book, after which Richard Benvenuto examines the struggle in Jane between her natural impulses and religious morality.

Feminist critic Nina Auerbach sees Rochester as Jane's projection, while the feminist poet Adrienne Rich plausibly argues that the insane Bertha Rochester is a realistic image of a fate that threatens Jane in her patriarchal and power-mad society.

The Marxist Terry Eagleton rather oddly finds Jane's spiritual autonomy to be an implicit critique of the class structure of her society, after which the historicist Nancy Pell also finds political implication in Jane Eyre's emotional condition. Sandra Gilbert and Susan Gubar, the dynamic duo of feminist criticism, read the novel's opening as an omen of emotional crises to come.

A powerful sense of both the importance of sexual initiation and its blocking agents in the novel is conveyed by John Maynard, while Tom Winnifrith devotes himself to autobiographical elements in *Jane Eyre*. Bettina L. Knapp interprets the red-room episode, after which Robert Kendrick reads Rochester's Christian conversion at the book's conclusion as a further retreat from patriarchy.

In the final extract, the biographer Lyndall Gordon broods upon the war between men and women in *Jane Eyre*.

Introduction

HAROLD BLOOM

Charlotte Brontë, particularly in *Jane Eyre,* manifests an aggressivity towards her readers that is infrequent among the major novelists. Though she professed great admiration for William Makepeace Thackeray, the author of *Vanity Fair,* he was not an authentic influence upon her. Like her sister Emily, the poet-novelist who composed *Wuthering Heights,* Charlotte was the perhaps involuntary disciple of the poet Lord Byron, whose personality and works are the inspiration for Rochester in *Jane Eyre* and for Heathcliff in *Wuthering Heights.* Charlotte's vengeance upon Byron is enacted both against her male readers and against Rochester. Byronic dramatization gives us not only Rochester, a pure type of the Byronic hero, but also "the Byronic pride and passion of Jane herself," in the words of the feminist critics Sandra M. Gilbert and Susan Gubar. The sexual intensity of Rochester is matched by that of Jane, whose relation to Rochester is a barely idealized version of Charlotte Brontë's permanent obsession with Lord Byron, who was at once the Ernest Hemingway and the Clark Gable of the Romantic era.

Rochester is all but castrated by Charlotte, since his maiming and blinding by the plot is so curiously gratuitous. If Gustave Flaubert can be said to murder Emma Bovary, while protesting that he *is* the lady, then it is perhaps true that Charlotte Brontë symbolically castrates Rochester, in the process of taming him into a mate suitable for Jane Eyre. As narrator, Jane scarcely can be distinguished from Charlotte, both sharing the same ferocity of will. The domestication of Rochester, while painful, is less spiritually sadistic than is his religious conversion, a kind of final indignity visited upon Byron's surrogate by the clergyman's daughter, Charlotte Brontë.

The critic Sylvère Monod observed that "Charlotte Brontë is thus led to bully her reader because she distrusts him." Substitute "Rochester" for "her reader" in that sentence, and it would be just as accurate. When the novel concludes, famously, by telling us: "Reader, I married him," it goes on to give us a peculiarly phrased idealization of the union of Jane Eyre and her battered husband:

> I have now been married ten years. I know what it is to live entirely for and with what I love best on earth. I hold myself supremely blest–blest beyond what language can express; because I am my husband's life as fully as he is mine. No woman was ever nearer to her mate than I am: absolutely more bone of his bone, and flesh of his flesh. I know no weariness of my Edward's society: he knows none of mine, any more than we do of the pulsation of the heart that beats in our separate bosoms; consequently, we are ever together. To be together is for us to be at once as free as in solitude, as gay as in company. We talk, I believe, all day long: to talk to each other is but an animated and audible thinking. All my confidence is bestowed on him; all his confidence is devoted to me: we are precisely suited in character; perfect concord is the result.

This is a radical new version of Adam and Eve: "bone of his bone, and flesh of his flesh." That "perfect concord" is more a total fusion than it is a harmony. We are reminded of Catherine Earnshaw's fierceness in *Wuthering Heights:* "I *am* Heathcliff." A marriage that is almost an ingestion defies the truth that even the most authentic eros unites only in act, not in essence. The drive, the will-to-power over life and the reader, is so consistently maintained by Charlotte Brontë that we do not resist her. Aesthetically, we have our reward, even if her heroine's triumph makes some male readers more than a little uneasy. ❖

Biography of Charlotte Brontë

Charlotte Brontë was born on April 21, 1816, to Patrick and Maria Brontë in Thornton, Lancashire, England. Patrick Brontë, an Irishman, published several undistinguished volumes of prose and verse and Maria Branwell Brontë, a Cornishwoman, demonstrated some literary ability in letters and an unpublished essay. Brontë supported his family, however, by obtaining the curacy of Haworth parish in 1820. A year later, Maria Brontë died, and an aunt took charge of the house and the children.

In 1824, Charlotte and three of her sisters—the two oldest, Maria and Elizabeth, and the younger Emily—were sent to the Clergy Daughters' School at Cowan Bridge. The harsh treatment they received at the boarding school, depicted as Lowood in *Jane Eyre,* contributed to the untimely death of Maria and Elizabeth. Charlotte and Emily then returned home to their father, their brother, Patrick Branwell, and their younger sister, Anne.

The four close-knit siblings spent their days wandering the surrounding Yorkshire moors and reading and writing voraciously. In 1826 their father brought home a box of wooden soldiers that inspired the children to write chronicles of an imaginary world called the Glasstown Confederacy. Gradually Charlotte, with the help of Branwell, channeled her creative energies into describing adventures in the exotic world Angria, while Emily, with the assistance of Anne, turned to the fantasy world Gondal. While Emily continually revisited Gondal in her poems, Charlotte composed *Farewell to Angria* when she was twenty-three.

When they reached adulthood, all three sisters reluctantly left Haworth for a time to become governesses. Preparing to open a school of their own, in 1842 Charlotte and Emily studied foreign languages at a boarding school in Brussels, Belgium, run by Monsieur and Madame Constantin Héger. In 1843, Charlotte became a teacher at the school but suffered from an impossible love for her married employer; the painful situation influenced her later writing.

Charlotte returned home in 1844, and by 1845 the whole family was reunited. Unable to launch their school, the sisters were distracted by domestic troubles; the Reverend Brontë was becoming older and weaker, and the once-talented Branwell was turning to alcohol and opium. However, the Brontë women remained undaunted in their literary ambitions. In 1846, Charlotte convinced Emily and Anne to join her in publishing the pseudonymous *Poems by Currer, Ellis, and Acton Bell.* Though the poetry collection received little notice, the sisters were already completing their first novels.

By 1847, the budding novelists realized mixed results with their works. Emily's *Wuthering Heights* and Anne's *Agnes Grey* were published, while Charlotte's *The Professor,* a rather lackluster account of a Brussels teacher and his marriage, was rejected. Charlotte overcame the disappointment with her next novel, *Jane Eyre,* published in 1847. The novel, a compelling story of a plain, independent governess who finds love under melodramatic circumstances, immediately earned acclaim. In contrast, her sisters' works did not attract much attention during their lifetime. Anne tried again in 1848, with the novel *The Tenant of Wildfell Hall.* When rumors circulated that *Tenant* was actually written by the best-selling Currer Bell, the sisters finally discarded their pseudonyms.

The family's enjoyment of its success was tragically brought to a halt in 1848. After the dissipated Branwell died in September, Emily and Anne caught consumption; Emily succumbed in December and Anne in May 1849. Battling ill health herself, Charlotte was left alone at Haworth to care for her aging father.

In her final years, Charlotte persevered in her writing. *Shirley,* a novel concerning a small country parish, was published in 1849. During this time, Charlotte occasionally sought relief from her depressing circumstances by traveling to London, where she socialized with other prominent writers, including William Makepeace Thackeray. While visiting friends in northern England in 1850, she was introduced to the novelist

Elizabeth Gaskell, who became her first biographer in 1857. Brontë's last novel, *Villette*—the story of an orphan who encounters love while making her own way as a teacher in Belgium—was published in 1853. A year later, she finally accepted Haworth curate Arthur Nicholls's proposal, and the two were married on June 19.

Charlotte Brontë died from pregnancy toxemia on March 31, 1855. *The Professor* (1857) and *Emma,* the fragment of a novel, were published posthumously, and interest in her earlier works continues unabated to this day. ❖

Thematic and Structural Analysis

The opening chapters of *Jane Eyre* describe Jane's early life at Gateshead with the Reed family, where, as an orphan, she is an unloved outsider and a victim of injustice and betrayal. Even the weather, a potent force throughout the story, reflects Jane's gloomy interior mood among the Reed family and their inhospitable attitude toward her: A "cold winter wind" and penetrating rain make taking a walk impossible (**chapter one**). The novel thus quickly establishes the central themes of isolation and the quest for personal power. The first-person narrative voice indicates that we will know only what Jane knows and that the perspective will be hers alone—and therefore both limited and controlling. Her powerlessness to overcome injustice and punishment is magnified by her status as an orphan, but, although small and physically vulnerable, Jane increasingly gains power over her circumstances. *Jane Eyre* is thus a woman's bildungsroman, a story of her passage from childhood to adulthood through a process of intellectual and emotional growth.

At the novel's opening, Jane, excluded from the family for an unstated crime until she may "acquire a more sociable and childlike disposition," retires with a book to a window seat, hidden behind draperies and protected from the icy rain by glass panes. Her cousin, fourteen-year-old John Reed, is a bully who calls her an "animal" and injures her with her book. When she violently retaliates she is locked in the "red-room," where images of confinement and hallucination tell an archetypal story of wrongful and horrifying punishment (**chapter two**). Puzzled by her position in the Reed family, she wonders, "Why could I never please?" In her misery, Jane is comforted by a belief that her uncle, had he lived, would have treated her with greater kindness than her aunt, Mrs. Reed. She imagines revenge in the form of her dead uncle "revisiting the earth" to "avenge the oppressed" Jane, a fantasy that will recur and be fulfilled later, when the family group disintegrates. The moonlight through the red-room blinds is steady, but—as Jane thinks of ghosts walking the earth—another seemingly phantom light is not. Her imagination activated, the child screams and the household quickly responds. Aunt Reed, with shocking heartlessness in the face of Jane's hysterical fear, locks her in again, whereupon the child faints.

In **chapter three** Jane wakes from her faint, back in her nursery bed and under the care of Bessie, a kind servant, and the apothecary, Mr. Lloyd. He asks her if she would rather live with other relations, but Mrs. Reed has already told Jane that the Eyres are all poor and "low." Jane has seen the poor and has no wish to live among them: She is "not heroic enough to purchase liberty at the price of caste." He suggests that she might like to go to school, and indeed Mrs. Reed is happy to send "the tiresome, ill-conditioned child" anywhere.

Mr. Brocklehurst, the head of Lowood Institution, a charity school for orphan girls, comes to Gateshead to interview Jane (**chapter four**). To the child he is an intimidating "black pillar," and Mrs. Reed ruins her hopeful anticipation of a fresh future by advising him that Jane "has a tendency to deceit." Brocklehurst promises to have her watched for signs of this damning defect, but later Jane retaliates against her aunt with a verbal assault in a "savage, high" voice in which she promises to broadcast the truth of her aunt's cruelty. Clearly, Jane is no self-effacing Cinderella. She is victorious, but the price is great. Her own hatred and vengeance affect her like a corrosive poison, and even nature reflects her subsequent spiritual vacancy in the "black frost," the "opaque sky," and the field whose short grass is "nipped and blanched."

Jane leaves Gateshead for Lowood in predawn darkness, just after a half-moon has set. (The moon permeates the text of *Jane Eyre* with pagan associations of the female, and the young woman will later draw strength from this mythic mother at Thornfield and, again, on the heath near Marsh End.) At Lowood, a school for girls of humble caste and ambition, the food is miserable and inadequate, the instruction rigid and by rote (**chapter five**). But for Jane it marks a place where she will gain strength, direction, and self-discipline.

Maria Temple, the superintendent, becomes a role model of compassion, intelligence, and restraint and encourages Jane's intellectual growth. Like all the women in the novel, she helps

Jane (either by emulation or by resistance) reach maturity and define a woman's limits and possibilities in nineteenth-century society. Along with Miss Temple, an older student named Helen Burns becomes a model for Jane. Helen, who will die of typhus in Jane's arms, is intellectually intense, deeply spiritual, and able to withstand the unjust severity of her instructors (**chapter six**). When Jane is hoisted upon the "pedestal of infamy" and Brocklehurst brands her a liar before the whole school (**chapter seven**), Helen counters Jane's despair by reminding her that her own conscience is all that matters and that she has no need to "sink overwhelmed with distress, when life is so soon over, and death is so certain an entrance to happiness—to glory." Jane is calmed but saddened by her friend's words. Helen's consuming spirituality is impossible for Jane, but her purity and erudition, together with Miss Temple's kindness and trust, inspire Jane "to pioneer [her] way through every difficulty" (**chapter eight**).

As winter withdraws, nature intervenes as a catalyst for both destruction and improvement (**chapters nine and ten**). Spring brings typhus and the death of many students, including the already weakened Helen Burns. Following the terrible outbreak, Lowood is taken over by more generous benefactors, and Jane remains to enjoy the benefits, first finishing her education, then staying on as a teacher. Miss Temple marries and is "lost" to Jane, but her departure causes Jane to consider a life away from Lowood. "I desired liberty," she recalls, but qualifies her desire, asking only that fate allow her "a new servitude." She places an ad for a position as governess, and Mrs. Fairfax of Thornfield engages her.

Of her arrival at Thornfield Jane recalls, with detached irony and some humor, that it seemed "a different region to Lowood, more populous, less picturesque: more stirring, less romantic"; Thornfield will in fact prove highly picturesque and intensely romantic (**chapter eleven**). At "the stroke of twelve" she follows Mrs. Fairfax through the "chill and vault-like air" of the mansion to a small room, pleasantly furnished in "ordinary modern style." She awakes to her new duties and a "fairer era of life." Her only regret is that she is small, pale, and has "features so irregular and so marked." On a tour of the house with Mrs. Fairfax, Jane presciently observes that the attic passageway resembles something one would expect to find in "Bluebeard's castle." She hears a "tragic" and "preternatural" laugh that Mrs. Fairfax attributes to a servant, Grace Poole. It is noon, a most unlikely time for terror, and Jane feels foolish for being surprised. The conversation turns at once to Adele Varens, Jane's young pupil, who is French born, charming, and immediately fond of her new governess—a figure who, having no "marked traits of character," seems to be primarily a literary device by which Jane may be acceptably brought into proximity with Thornfield's owner, Edward Rochester.

"Anybody may blame me who likes," Jane remarks in **chapter twelve**, challenging the reader to criticize her restless desire for more wide-ranging life experiences. Gateshead, Lowood, and now even Thornfield confine her like prisons. She restlessly paces, dwelling on various tales her "imagination created, and narrated continuously; quickened with all of incident, life, fire, feeling" not yet part of her experience. But Grace Poole's terrible laugh is frequent and disturbing, so Jane is happy to escape to post a letter for Mrs. Fairfax.

The barren fields and trees in the pale, late afternoon sunlight please her by their "utter solitude and leafless repose." The moon rises, and the sounds of a horse and dog rapidly approaching on Hay Lane evoke her childhood dread of the "Gytrash," a spirit figuring in Bessie's nursery stories. Both horse and rider suddenly slip upon the ice-covered road in front of her, prompting what Jane primly suspects is a volley of curses from the rider. In this moment between daylight and moonlight, she is not afraid of the stranger. The "frown, the roughness of the traveller, set me at my ease," she explains, but he refuses her assistance. Although it is "an incident of no moment, no romance, no interest," she is intrigued. She returns to Thornfield and, seeing there the dog she had thought a Gytrash, realizes that the man was Rochester.

To Jane's thinking Thornfield is much improved by the presence of "a master," and, as the household gathers in the drawing room that evening (**chapter thirteen**), she observes Rochester most critically. He is neither tall nor handsome nor graceful, but his features are somehow harmonious. He seems to take little notice of Jane, which puts her at ease to enjoy his "eccentricity." After a moment he quizzes Jane on her background, and she answers simply and without elaboration. He then remarks on her "look of another world," suggests that she may have been waiting for fairies when he met her on Hay Lane, accuses her of bewitching his horse, dismisses her meager talent at the piano, and asks instead to see her drawings. Jane's sketches and paintings are remarkable for their psychological intensity. She admits to Rochester that she was "tormented" by her inability to draw more exactly what she had imagined. Rochester is an incisive critic who perceives both the works' slight weaknesses and the complexity and intelligence of their artist. When he ends the evening abruptly, Jane presses Mrs. Fairfax for more information about their employer and learns only that Rochester "shuns" Thornfield because of an unhappy relationship with his deceased father and older brother.

In **chapters fourteen and fifteen** Jane and Rochester probe each other's character with considerable rhetorical flair. What torments Rochester Jane cannot yet know, but she responds to his rambling and unspecific confession of degeneracy with clarity and reason. "You are human and fallible," she reminds him, as she attempts to extricate herself from "a discourse that was all darkness" to her. Rochester tells Jane of his liaison with the mother of Adele, Celine Varens, a "French opera-dancer" who had bartered her affection for money. "The more you and I converse, the better; for while I cannot blight you, you may refresh me," he tells her, unaware of the complex irony of his words. She considers the intimacy of their conversations and wonders at her "power to amuse him." Jane begins to love Rochester, though she yet admits only that "his presence in the room was more cheering than the brightest fire."

"Goblin-laughter" disturbs Jane's sleep after this musing about Rochester (**chapter fifteen**), and she wonders if the "unnatural sound" is Grace Poole "possessed by a devil." Footsteps recede to the third floor, and Jane opens her bedroom door to find a lighted candle on the rug. Although "surprised" and "amazed," Jane is a creature of action, and her purpose at this moment is to find Mrs. Fairfax. When she sees smoke coming from Rochester's door, all else is forgotten as she enters quickly to put out the fire in his bed. Overcome by smoke, he is unresponsive until Jane has "baptized" him with all the water she can find. He admonishes her to say nothing of the incident and quickly blames Grace Poole. Jane moves to leave him, but he stops her, holding her hand in both of his and puzzling her with the "strange fire in his look." **Chapter sixteen** brings daylight but no illumination to the mystery. Jane is surprised to find Grace Poole busy repairing the damage to Rochester's room and can make no sense of either Grace's enigmatic character or her true position at Thornfield.

Jane considers, with some satisfaction, the character of her relationship with Rochester. She ponders the "pleasure of vexing and soothing him by turns." They are intellectual equals, and she happily anticipates their continued conversation. But the mood abruptly changes when she learns that Rochester has left Thornfield for the company of the "elegant young" Ingram girls—in particular, the accomplished and "noble"-featured Blanche Ingram. All appetite gone, Jane chastises herself as a "fool" for having "rejected the real" and "rabidly devoured the ideal." When Rochester returns with the Ingram family (**chapter seventeen**), Jane tries to gauge whether or not Blanche "were such as [she] should fancy likely to suit Mr Rochester's taste." Blanche is tall, beautiful, and "dark as a Spaniard," and Jane becomes acutely conscious of her own love for Rochester as he enters the room, seemingly unaware of her presence: "He made me love him without looking at me." Although he ignores her in company, he later hurries after her when she discreetly leaves, and insists that she appear before his guests every night.

At an evening party with the Ingrams from which Rochester is absent, a mysterious gypsy fortune teller appears at the house and is brought in to entertain the guests (**chapter eighteen**). The old woman, who is clearly a member of the household in disguise, suggests to Jane that she would do well to show more affection to Rochester. The gypsy probes Jane's responses to determine the depth of her feeling for him and advises her to take the happiness that is near her. When the old woman at last removes the disguise Jane is surprised, not that the gypsy is a fraud, which she already suspected, but that the one disguised is not the mysterious Grace Poole but instead Rochester himself. Regaining her composure, she tells him that a stranger named Mason, from the West Indies, arrived at

Thornfield that morning. Rochester is stunned and, imagining a future scenario in which he is ostracized by his society guests, asks Jane if she too would "dare censure" for his sake. This seems to her a rhetorical question, and she replies that she would (**chapter nineteen**).

Awakened that night by the "glorious gaze" of the moon upon her, Jane is next startled by a single "savage" cry from the third floor (**chapter twenty**). Rochester, descending from the upper region with a candle, reassures the guests, telling them that a servant has had a nightmare. He asks Jane's help and brings her to a third-floor room where Mason lies bleeding, attacked by someone now locked in an inner room, who Jane thinks must be Grace Poole. As Mason is bandaged he discloses that he was bitten by an unidentified "she" who "sucked the blood . . . and said she'd drain his heart." Once Mason has been restored and has departed, Rochester walks with Jane in the cool garden. He asks her to imagine herself as a wild, spoiled boy and tells a story of youthful bad judgment and worse attachment. The story perplexes her, and Rochester sardonically asks her if she will sit up with him the night before he marries Blanche.

In **chapter twenty-one** Jane returns to Gateshead to oversee the dissolution of the Reed family and the death of her aunt—an episode that fulfills her childhood revenge fantasy in the red-room. John Reed has committed suicide after squandering his estate; his mother is dying of a stroke; Georgiana is "very plump" and useless, eventually to marry a dissipated gentleman; and the cold Eliza is leaving for a nunnery. Jane is also in transition: Convinced that Rochester is lost to her, she feels once more "a wanderer on the face of the earth." The passion of childhood resentment has been replaced by a compassion for human weakness and a desire for love and spiritual wholeness. Mrs. Reed, on the other hand, still hates Jane. But in some remorse, she gives Jane a letter that she has hidden for three years, advising the orphan that John Eyre of Madeira, Jane's uncle, wished to send for her and adopt her. It seems of little importance to Jane at this point.

Jane returns to Thornfield, grieving that she must advertise for another position because Rochester will soon be married (**chapter twenty-two**). A "fortnight of dubious calm" follows her return, in which there is no hint of a forthcoming wedding. Yet Rochester allows the tormenting fiction to continue— reminding Jane that she and "little Adele had better trot forth- with." Only after he has tortured her to tears does he suddenly name Jane as his intended bride (**chapter twenty-three**). By then, he must work hard to convince her that his words are true. She asks that he turn his face toward the moonlight so that she may "read" it more clearly, and then, seeing his own suffering at the thought that she might indeed leave, she accepts his proposal. Mrs. Fairfax is perplexed and cold to the news, reminding Jane that men "in his station" do not marry their governesses. But Jane's strong love for Rochester admits no doubt, and nothing greater. At the end of **chapter twenty- four** she observes that he stands "like an eclipse" between her and "every thought of religion." She cannot "see God for His creature: of whom [she] had made an idol."

Disturbing dreams merge with reality on the nights before her wedding (**chapter twenty-five**). Jane tells Rochester about an encounter, not a dream, as terrifying as any nightmare. A tall, dark woman with swollen lips and bloodshot eyes tears Jane's wedding veil and comes close to her face with "fiery eyes." Jane faints from terror, the second time she has ever done so. The hysterical child in the red-room at Gateshead has become a rational woman, but she can no better analyze this foul apparition than she could the specter in her childhood. Rochester tells her it must have been Grace Poole, and there seems to Jane no other possibility.

The wedding is a disaster. The ceremony is shockingly inter- rupted by the disclosure, by Mason and his agent, that Rochester already has a wife, Mason's sister, living at Thornfield (**chapter twenty-six**). Rochester takes Jane, Mason, and others at the ceremony to the third-floor room where they see Bertha Rochester, the lunatic for whom Grace Poole is the caretaker. The woman, who is almost as tall as her husband, "corpulent" and "virile," attacks him, biting his cheek. She is everything that Jane is not—yet her dark double. Bertha Rochester is an extreme of unrestrained physicality and passion, a Victorian female run amok. That she is foreign accentuates her difference from Jane, but her uncontrolled acts are a warning of the danger to Jane in surrendering herself to physical passion. Jane returns to her room and bolts herself in. In her intense anguish, in which her life and prospects now seem desolate, she experiences an epiphany: "a remembrance of God." She must leave Thornfield to preserve her spiritual self.

Yet Rochester tells her his story and asks her to live with him as lover, if not wife. The temptation of romantic love almost exhausts her strength, but not quite (**chapter twenty-seven**). That night, Jane dreams of the red-room and of the moon that suddenly speaks to her spirit: "My daughter, flee temptation." She wakes and responds, "Mother, I will."

A coach takes her as far as Whitcross, a desolate crossroads ten miles from the nearest town (**chapter twenty-eight**). Having lost what little money she had brought with her and anxious to avoid questioning, Jane walks the heath, a motherless child who imagines herself nature's child. The night is mild and God seems everywhere; Jane consoles herself with the idea that he will surely comfort Rochester as well as herself.

The following morning, weak from hunger and exposure, Jane approaches a parsonage, but the housekeeper turns her away, explaining that the clergyman is at Marsh End and cannot help her. Cold and rain bring her to desperation by the next day, and she devours some cold porridge a little girl is about to feed to pigs. She expects to die before the next day, but the thought that Rochester still lives sustains her. She follows a distant light to the cottage at Marsh End, where she is taken in by the Rivers family.

Chapters twenty-nine through thirty-five describe Jane's sojourn at Marsh End. The Rivers women are educated, intelligent, and inquisitive. Jane notes that their natures dovetail beautifully with her own and that "mutual affection—of the strongest kind—[is] the result." Their clergyman brother, St. John, is intensely focused upon his spiritual vocation, but "pure-lived, conscientious, zealous as he [is]—he [has] not yet found that peace of God which passeth all understanding" (**chapter thirty**). Neither has Jane, who, believing them to have similar spiritual longings, is sympathetic to his struggle and his suffering.

The death of their father and the evident loss of income require Diana and Mary to leave to become governesses. St. John finds her a teaching position, and Jane reasons that, because she will be independent and the job is not "mentally degrading," she may "save [her other accomplishments] till they are wanted. They will keep." St. John will embark for Eastern missionary work. Diana remarks that her brother is "inexorable as death" in his vocation and willing to sacrifice all "natural affection." But before pursuing their separate missions, the Rivers women learn of the death of a distant uncle, their last hope, who has left them no money and thus no reprieve from their scattering.

Jane moves into her "little room with whitewashed walls," where she feels both "desolate" and "degraded," the sisters depart, and St. John continues to prepare for the missions (**chapters thirty-one and thirty-two**). He tells Jane that he must overcome "a last conflict with human weakness," his natural affection for the lovely Rosamond Oliver, the daughter of the school's benefactor. Jane encourages him to balance his vocation with the inclinations of his heart—perhaps to work locally. But his "great work" consumes everything. Jane counsels him against such sacrifice and is baffled when he proclaims himself a "cold, hard man."

In **chapter thirty-three** St. John learns Jane's identity and confronts her. He tells her that Rochester advertised for her whereabouts and that a solicitor wrote to St. John about her disappearance from Thornfield. He also tells her that the Rivers' dead uncle was the same Mr. Eyre of Madeira whom Mrs. Reed had revealed to Jane. The Rivers inherit nothing from him, but Jane inherits a fortune of twenty thousand pounds. Jane divides the inheritance among them, and the family reunites at Marsh End. Domestic intimacy allows an intense relationship to develop between Jane and St. John that will tempt her to abandon her desire for her own vocation and take St. John's as her own. "By degrees," she notes (**chapter thirty-four**), "he acquired a certain influence over me that took away my liberty of mind. . . . I fell under a freezing spell."

But all the while, the idea of Rochester—"not a vapour sunshine could dispel"—haunts Jane. His sexuality contrasts strongly with St. John's "Greek face" and his marblelike, "experiment" kiss. Jane writes to the solicitor and to Mrs. Fairfax for any information about Rochester, but when the solicitor says he knows nothing and Mrs. Fairfax does not respond, she gives up hope.

To her surprise, St. John then asks Jane to accompany him to India as his wife. Jane could embrace missionary work as her vocation, but she rejects the martyrdom of marriage to a man who would "scrupulously observe" the "forms of love" without any love at all. To follow him on his terms would be a form of suicide, but she would, she says, go as a sister. St. John counters with Christian rhetorical weaponry that deeply upsets Jane. "And yet St John is a good man," Diana remarks later, when she and Jane discuss the impossibility of complying with his demands. When he acts toward her not as a lover but as "a guardian angel" watching over her soul, his sincerity seems to "subdue and rule" her, and she almost yields to the temptation to define—and lose—herself in his vocation. She compares her rejection of moral compromise with Rochester to her rejection of St. John, now. "To have yielded then would have been an error of principle; to [yield] now would [be] an error of judgment."

St. John's gentleness toward Jane in their final confrontation almost overwhelms her; even the room seems "full of visions." The commonsensical Jane keeps in mind that she knows what love is and that what St. John so passionately offers is only "almost" love. But duty may be worth as much—if God would make her path clear. She asks Heaven for some sign and warns the reader that what happens next may be either telepathy or hysteria—for she then hears Rochester call her name, and her dilemma is instantly resolved: "It was my time to assume ascendancy." She dismisses St. John, locks the door, says a prayer of thanks, and waits for daylight and her journey to Thornfield.

But Jane arrives to find Thornfield burned out and abandoned (**chapter thirty-six**). The innkeeper in town, who does not know her, tells the story of a young governess, a lunatic wife, and a thwarted marriage. By a lapse of gin-drinking Grace Poole, Bertha Rochester escaped and set fire to the house and threw herself off the battlements as Rochester tried to save her. He himself was blinded and lost a hand in the disaster. He lives isolated at Ferndean, thirty miles away, in the care of two servants. Jane has heard of the place, a manor house used as a hunting lodge by the Rochesters; she hires a chaise and hurries to reach Ferndean before dark.

The house at Ferndean is hidden by a dense tangle of foliage (**chapter thirty-seven**). Jane enters a barren clearing through a small gate. Rochester, like a "caged eagle" or a "sightless Samson," emerges from the manor, and Jane's anguish at seeing him so damaged keeps her quiet. Gradually she reveals her identity, and Rochester thinks she is a "delusion," a "sweet madness." She tells him that she has come to stay and that she is "quite rich." Jane may now marry on her own terms. When he asks if there were "only ladies in the house" where she has been, Jane is delighted that in the new balance of power the ability to "[fret] him out of his melancholy" resides with her.

"Reader, I married him." In Jane's most famous assertion the tale achieves resolution (**chapter thirty-eight**). Jane accepts a vocation in an unusual marriage. By his mutilation and dependence upon her, marriage becomes Rochester's vocation, too. But there are clear limits to their marriage. They are equals, but a cruel irony undercuts their equality: Mutilation and isolation are necessary to their happiness. Rochester may not be precisely castrated, but he is surely hobbled and will never again participate in the social life that has excluded Jane. Rochester is a Byronic figure made human, and their intense and romantic union is possible only in charmed seclusion. Jane reveals that the events narrated are ten years past, during which time they have had a son and Rochester has regained enough vision to walk without being led.

Jane ends her narrative with the conclusion to the story of St. John Rivers. He is a missionary in India, unmarried, and nearing death. Jane describes her "human tears" and "divine joy," certain that his hope for paradise will be realized. For St. John, it is the happiest possible ending. For Jane, however, an earthly paradise is enough. ❖

—*Tenley Williams*
New York University

List of Characters

Jane Eyre is the narrator and protagonist of the novel, a penniless orphan who eventually realizes her vocation in a marriage of high caste and unusual equality. Without money, known family connections, or beauty, she is educated to become a governess, thereby fulfilling a nineteenth-century convention. But, because of her intelligence, her passionate nature, and, paradoxically, her lack of family claims and restraints, Jane is free to imagine a life of greater experience and intensity in which to enjoy her intellectual gifts. She relies upon her own force of character and will to overcome the lopsided power relations of Victorian society, resisting victimization among the Reed family; self-immolation on the model of Helen Burns; ethical compromise in the romantic love of Edward Rochester; and spiritual self-effacement within St. John Rivers's religious vocation. In a novel permeated with bad weather, pagan and Christian imagery, and considerable physical and psychological stress, Jane Eyre perseveres to achieve a marriage of highly romantic love, intellectual equality, and physical passion.

Edward Rochester is the master of Thornfield, where Jane is employed as a governess when she leaves Lowood Institution. He is a Byronic figure—dark, brooding, volatile, and erotic. Jane observes that, while he is not handsome, his features are somehow harmonious and pleasing to her. He is a lonely and tormented man, though popular and sociable among his upper-class peers. Although of a different class, he is intrigued by Jane's forthright wit and intelligence, and their mutual attraction and regard becomes highly charged, romantic love. Their first wedding ceremony is halted by the disclosure that he has a lunatic wife, but when Jane finally returns to him—after his mutilation and her financial ascent—their physical and spiritual love for each other is undiminished, and they meet each other as equals.

St. John Rivers is Jane's cousin who saves her from death on the heath at Marsh End. He is a clergyman and a Christian zealot who tempts her to bury her desire for a vocation within his own as a missionary in India. He is classically handsome and as cold as a statue in matters of the heart. His beauty and sterility are the opposite of Rochester's rugged and erotic physicality. Jane is drawn to St. John because she recognizes in him her own spiritual longings. She senses that he denies his natural tenderness by an excess of Christian piety and purpose. She almost capitulates to his spiritual intensity, but the lack of physical love finally turns her away from him.

Bertha Rochester is the woman Rochester married in the West Indies as a young man, and who subsequently became mad. Locked in a third-floor room, she laughs preternaturally, disturbing and puzzling Jane until her existence is revealed and Rochester takes Jane to see the violent and wild specter that is his wife. After Jane leaves Thornfield, Bertha starts the fire that destroys the house and mutilates Rochester. She is an example and a confirmation of the dangers of untempered passion and physicality.

Maria Temple is the superintendent of Lowood Institution. Her intelligence, kindness, and gentility guide the lonely Jane into a circumspect and realistic young womanhood. They are friends and become colleagues at the school. When Miss Temple leaves Lowood to be married, Jane feels it as a personal loss.

Helen Burns is a highly intelligent and deeply spiritual student at Lowood, who is a favorite of Maria Temple and of Jane. She counsels Jane against indulging in anger and dwelling upon personal injustice and indignity. She endures the cruelties of illness and the school as if already on her way to an otherworldly paradise. Helen inspires Jane by her strength but saddens her by her self-immolation. She dies of typhus.

Diana and Mary Rivers, with their brother, St. John, compose a family for Jane. They are bluestockings, nineteenth-century women who are well read and strong in their ideas and opinions. Jane is happy in their company at Marsh End and happier still to share with them her inheritance from the uncle who, coincidentally, was uncle to them all.

Grace Poole is hired by Rochester to care for Bertha Rochester in the third-floor room. For months, Jane attributes the disturbing laugh she hears to Grace, not suspecting any other possibility. After the fire in Rochester's room, which he tells her is the work of Grace, Jane is confounded by the continued presence of this coarse-featured, gin-drinking enigma.

Adele Varens, the product of Rochester's liaison with a French singer who exchanged her affection for money, is the young child for whom Jane is hired as governess at Thornfield. ❖

Critical Views

Henry F. Chorley on the Power of *Jane Eyre*

[Henry F. Chorley (1808–1872) was a prolific fiction writer, playwright, librettist, and music and literary critic. Among his works are *Memorials of Mrs. Hemans* (1836), *The Authors of England* (1838), and *Modern German Music* (1854). In this review of *Jane Eyre,* Chorley attests to the emotive power of *Jane Eyre* as well as its realism.]

There is so much power in this novel as to make us overlook certain eccentricities in the invention, which trench in one or two places on what is improbable, if not unpleasant. Jane Eyre is an orphan thrown upon the protection—or, to speak correctly, the cruelty—of relations living in an out-of-the-way corner of England; who neglect, maltreat, chastize, and personally abuse her. She becomes dogged, revengeful, superstitious: and at length, after a scene,—which we hope is out of nature now that "the Iron Rule" is over-ruled and the reign of the tribe Squeers ended,—the child turns upon her persecutors with such precocious power to threaten and alarm, that they condemn her to an *oubliette*—sending her out of the house to a so-called charitable institution. There she has again to prove wretchedness, hard fare, and misconstruction. The trial, however, is this time not unaccompanied by more gracious influences. Jane Eyre is taught, by example, that patience is nobler than passion; and so far as we can gather from her own confessions, grows up into a plain, self-sustained young woman, with a capital of principle sufficient to regulate those more dangerous gifts which the influences of her childhood had so exasperated. Weary of the monotonous life of a teacher, she advertises for the situation of a governess; and is engaged into an establishment—singular, but not without prototype—to take care of the education of the French ward of a country gentleman; which said girl proves, when called by her right name, to be the child of an opera *danseuse*. The pretty, frivolous, little faëry Adele, with her hereditary taste for dress, coquetry, and pantomimic grace, is true to life. Perhaps, too—we dare not speak more positively—there is truth in the abrupt, strange, clever Mr.

Rochester; and in the fearless, original way in which the strong man and the young governess travel over each other's minds till, in a puzzled and uncomfortable manner enough, they come to a mutual understanding. Neither is the mystery of Thornfield an exaggeration of reality. We, ourselves, know of a large mansion-house in a distant county where, for many years, a miscreant was kept in close confinement,—and his existence, at best, only darkly hinted in the neighbourhood. Some such tale as this was told in a now-forgotten novel—*Sketches of a Seaport Town*. We do not quarrel with the author of *Jane Eyre* for the manner in which he has made the secret explode at a critical juncture of the story. From that point forward, however, we think the heroine is too outrageously tried, and too romantically assisted in her difficulties:—until arrives the last moment, at which obstacles fall down like the battlements of *Castle Melodrame*, in the closing scene, when "avenging thunder strikes the towers of Crime, and far above in Heaven's etherial light young Hymen's flower-decked temple shines revealed." No matter, however:—as exciting strong interest of its old-fashioned kind *Jane Eyre* deserves high praise, and commendation to the novel-reader who prefers story to philosophy, pedantry, or Puseyite controversy.

—Henry F. Chorley, [Review of *Jane Eyre*], *Athenaeum*, 23 October 1847, pp. 1100–1101

EDWIN P. WHIPPLE ON THE MORALITY OF *JANE EYRE*

[Edwin P. Whipple (1819–1886) was one of the leading American literary critics and reviewers of the nineteenth century. Among his many books are *Essays and Reviews* (1848) and *The Literature of the Age of Elizabeth* (1869). In this review of *Jane Eyre*, Whipple (who also unfavorably reviewed Emily Brontë's *Wuthering Heights*) remarks on the popularity of the novel in the United States but expresses reservations on its moral message.]

Not many months ago, the New England States were visited by a distressing mental epidemic, passing under the name of the "Jane Eyre fever," which defied all the usual nostrums of the established doctors of criticism. Its effects varied with different constitutions, in some producing a soft ethical sentimentality, which relaxed all the fibres of conscience, and in others exciting a general fever of moral and religious indignation. It was to no purpose that the public were solemnly assured, through the intelligent press, that the malady was not likely to have any permanent effect either on the intellectual or moral constitution. The book which caused the distemper would probably have been inoffensive, had not some sly manufacturer of mischief hinted that it was a book which no respectable man should bring into his family circle. Of course, every family soon had a copy of it, and one edition after another found eager purchasers. The hero, Mr. Rochester, (not the same person who comes to so edifying an end in the pages of Dr. Gilbert Burnet,) became a great favorite in the boarding-schools and in the worshipful society of governesses. That portion of Young America known as ladies' men began to swagger and swear in the presence of the gentler sex, and to allude darkly to events in their lives which excused impudence and profanity.

The novel of *Jane Eyre,* which caused this great excitement, purports to have been edited by Currer Bell, and the said Currer divides the authorship, if we are not misinformed, with a brother and sister. The work bears the marks of more than one mind and one sex, and has more variety than either of the novels which claim to have been written by Acton Bell. The family mind is strikingly peculiar, giving a strong impression of unity, but it is still male and female. From the masculine tone of *Jane Eyre,* it might pass altogether as the composition of a man, were it not for some unconscious feminine peculiarities, which the strongest-minded woman that ever aspired after manhood cannot suppress. These peculiarities refer not only to elaborate descriptions of dress, and the minutiæ of the sick-chamber, but to various superficial refinements of feeling in regard to the external relations of the sex. It is true that the noblest and best representations of female character have been produced by men; but there are niceties of thought and emotion in a woman's mind which no man can delineate, but which often escape unawares from a female writer. There are numerous examples of these in *Jane Eyre.* The leading characteristic of the novel, however, and the secret of its charm, is the clear, distinct, decisive style of its representation of character, manners, and scenery; and this continually suggests a male mind. In the earlier chapters, there is little, perhaps, to break the impression that we are reading the autobiography of a powerful and peculiar female intellect; but when the admirable Mr. Rochester appears, and the profanity, brutality, and slang of the misanthropic profligate give their torpedo shocks to the nervous system,—and especially when we are favored with more than one scene given to the exhibition of mere animal appetite, and to courtship after the manner of kangaroos and the heroes of Dryden's plays,—we are gallant enough to detect the hand of a gentleman in the composition. There are also scenes of passion, so hot, emphatic, and condensed in expression, and so sternly masculine in feeling, that we are almost sure we observe the mind of the author of *Wuthering Heights* at work in the text.

The popularity of *Jane Eyre* was doubtless due in part to the freshness, raciness, and vigor of mind it evinced; but it was obtained not so much by these qualities as by frequent dealings in moral paradox, and by the hardihood of its assaults upon the prejudices of proper people. Nothing causes more delight, at least to one third of every community, than a successful attempt to wound the delicacy of their scrupulous neighbours, and a daring peep into regions which acknowledge the authority of no conventional rules. The authors of *Jane Eyre* have not accomplished this end without an occasional violation of probability and considerable confusion of plot and character, and they have made the capital mistake of supposing that an artistic representation of character and manners is a literal imitation of individual life. The consequence is, that in dealing with vicious personages they confound vulgarity with truth, and awaken too often a feeling of unmitigated disgust. The writer who colors too warmly the degrading scenes through which his immaculate hero passes is rightly held as an equivocal teacher of purity; it is not by the bold expression of blasphemy and ribaldry that a great novelist conveys the most truthful idea of the misanthropic and the dissolute. The truth is, that the whole firm of Bell & Co. seem to have a sense of the depravity of human nature peculiarly their own. It is the yahoo, not the demon, that they select for representation; their Pandemonium is of mud rather than fire.

—Edwin P. Whipple, "Novels of the Season," *North American Review* No. 141 (October 1848): 355–57

LADY EASTLAKE ON THE DEPRAVITY OF *JANE EYRE*

[Elizabeth Rigby, Lady Eastlake (1809–1893), was a music and art critic who wrote *Letters from the Shores of the Baltic* (1842) and *Five Great Painters* (1883). Her *Journals and Correspondence* was published in 1895. In this review of *Jane Eyre,* Lady Eastlake strongly condemns the novel for its depravity and its anti-Christian sentiments.]

Jane Eyre is throughout the personification of an unregenerate and undisciplined spirit, the more dangerous to exhibit from that prestige of principle and self-control which is liable to dazzle the eye too much for it to observe the inefficient and unsound foundation on which it rests. It is true Jane does right, and exerts great moral strength, but it is the strength of a mere heathen mind which is a law unto itself. No Christian grace is perceptible upon her. She has inherited in fullest measure the worst sin of our fallen nature—the sin of pride. Jane Eyre is proud, and therefore she is ungrateful too. It pleased God to make her an orphan, friendless, and penniless—yet she thanks nobody, and least of all Him, for the food and raiment, the friends, companions, and instructors of her helpless youth—for the care and education vouchsafed to her till she was capable in mind as fitted in years to provide for herself. On the contrary, she looks upon all that has been done for her not only as her undoubted right, but as falling far short of it. The doctrine of humility is not more foreign to her mind than it is repudiated by her heart. It is by her own talents, virtues, and courage, that she is made to attain the summit of human happiness, and, as far as Jane Eyre's own statement is concerned, no one would think that she owed anything either to God above or to man below. She flees from Mr. Rochester, and has not a being to turn to. Why was this? The excellence of the present institution at Casterton, which succeeded that of Cowan Bridge near Kirkby Lonsdale—these being distinctly, as we hear, the original and the reformed Lowoods of the book—is pretty generally known. Jane had lived there for eight years with 110 girls and 15 teachers. Why had she formed no friendship among them? Other orphans have left the same and similar institutions, furnished with friends for life, and puzzled with homes to choose from. How comes it that Jane had acquired neither? Among that number of associates there were surely some exceptions to what she so presumptuously stigmatises as 'the society of inferior minds.' Of course it suited the author's end to represent the heroine as utterly destitute of the common means of assistance, in order to exhibit both her trials and her powers of self-support—the whole book rests on this assumption—but it is one which, under the circumstances, is very unnatural and very unjust.

Altogether the autobiography of Jane Eyre is preeminently an anti-Christian composition. There is throughout it a murmuring against the comforts of the rich and against the privations of the poor, which, as far as each individual is concerned, is a murmuring against God's appointment—there is a proud and perpetual assertion of the rights of man, for which we find no authority either in God's word or in God's providence—there is that pervading tone of ungodly discontent which is at once the most prominent and the most subtle evil which the law and the pulpit, which all civilized society in fact, has at the present day to contend with. We do not hesitate to say that the tone of mind and thought which has overthrown authority and violated every code human and divine abroad, and fostered Chartism and rebellion at home, is the same which has also written Jane Eyre.

Still we say again this is a very remarkable book. We are painfully alive to the moral, religious, and literary deficiencies of the picture, and such passages of beauty and power as we have quoted cannot redeem it, but it is impossible not to be spellbound with the freedom of the touch. It would be mere hackneyed courtesy to call it 'fine writing.' It bears no impress of being written at all, but is poured out rather in the heat and hurry of an instinct, which flows ungovernably on to its object, indifferent by what means it reaches it, and unconscious too. As regards the author's chief object, however, it is a failure—that, namely, of making a plain, odd woman, destitute of all the conventional features of feminine attraction, interesting in our sight. We deny that he has succeeded in this. Jane Eyre, in spite of some grand things about her, is a being totally uncongenial to our feelings from beginning to end. We acknowledge her firmness—we respect her determination—we feel for her struggles; but, for all that, and setting aside higher considerations, the impression she leaves on our mind is that of a decidedly vulgar-minded woman—one whom we should not care for as an acquaintance, whom we should not seek as a friend, whom we should not desire for a relation, and whom we should scrupulously avoid for a governess.

—Elizabeth Rigby (Lady Eastlake), [Review of *Jane Eyre*], *Quarterly Review* No. 167 (December 1848): 172–74

ALGERNON CHARLES SWINBURNE ON THE FLAWS AND VIRTUES OF *JANE EYRE*

[Algernon Charles Swinburne (1837–1909), aside from being a preeminent British poet of the later nineteenth century, was a prolific critic who did much to popularize the work of the Elizabethan dramatists. In this extract from *A Note on Charlotte Brontë* (1877), Swinburne acknowledges some flaws in the plot and execution of *Jane Eyre* but claims that these are dwarfed by the novel's great virtue—the portrayal of character.]

Take the first work of her genius in its ripe fullness and freshness of new fruit; a twig or two is twisted or blighted of the noble tree, a bud or so has been nipped or cankered by adverse winds or frost; but root and branch and bole are all straight and strong and solid and sound in grain. Whatever in

Jane Eyre is other than good is also less than important. The accident which brings a famished wanderer to the door of unknown kinsfolk might be a damning flaw in a novel of mere incident; but incident is not the keystone and commonplace is not the touchstone of this. The vulgar insolence and brutish malignity of the well-born guests at Thornfield Hall are grotesque and incredible in speakers of their imputed station; these are the natural properties of that class of persons which then supplied, as it yet supplies, the writers of such articles as one of memorable infamy and imbecility on *Jane Eyre* to the artistic and literary department of the *Quarterly Review.* So gross and grievous a blunder would entail no less than ruin on a mere novel of manners; but accuracy in the distinction and reproduction of social characteristics is not the test of capacity for such work as this. That test is only to be found in the grasp and manipulation of manly and womanly character. And, to my mind, the figure of Edward Rochester in this book remains, and seems like to remain, one of the only two male figures of wholly truthful workmanship and vitally heroic mould ever carved and coloured by a woman's hand. The other it is superfluous to mention; all possible readers will have uttered before I can transcribe the name of Paul Emanuel.

—Algernon Charles Swinburne, *A Note on Charlotte Brontë* (London: Chatto & Windus, 1877), pp. 26–28

LESLIE STEPHEN ON BRONTË'S DEFIANCE OF CONVENTIONALITY

[Leslie Stephen (1832–1904), the father of Virginia Woolf, was a distinguished critic and essayist. Among his major works are *History of English Thought in the Eighteenth Century* (1876) and *Hours in a Library* (1874–79). In this extract (originally a review of Swinburne's *A Note on Charlotte Brontë*), Stephen finds that the chief point of Brontë's work as a whole, and of *Jane Eyre* in particular, is a defiance of conventionality.]

One great aim of the writing, explained in the preface to the second edition of *Jane Eyre,* is a protest against conventionality. But the protest is combined with a most unflinching adherence to the proper conventions of society; and we are left in great doubt as to where the line ought to be drawn. Where does the unlawful pressure of society upon the individual begin, and what are the demands which it may rightfully make upon our respect? At one moment in *Jane Eyre* we seem to be drifting towards the solution that strong passion is the one really good thing in the world, and that all human conventions which oppose it should be disregarded. This was the tendency which shocked the respectable reviewers of the time. Of course they should have seen that the strongest sympathy of the author goes with the heroic self-conquest of the heroine under temptation. She triumphs at the cost of a determined self-sacrifice, and undoubtedly we are meant to sympathise with the martyr. Yet it is also true that we are left with the sense of an unsolved discord. Sheer stoical regard for duty is represented as something repulsive, however imposing, in the figure of St. John Rivers, and virtue is rewarded by the arbitrary removal of the obstacles which made it unpleasant. What would Jane Eyre have done, and what would our sympathies have been, had she found that Mrs. Rochester had not been burnt in the fire at Thornfield? That is rather an awkward question. Duty is supreme, seems to be the moral of the story; but duty sometimes involves a strain almost too hard for mortal faculties.

—Leslie Stephen, "Charlotte Brontë" (1877), *Hours in a Library* (1874–79; rev. ed. New York: G. P. Putnam's Sons, 1904), Vol. 3, pp. 306–7

AUGUSTINE BIRRELL ON THE VITALITY OF *JANE EYRE*

[Augustine Birrell (1850–1933) was a prolific British critic. He wrote several collections of essays and reviews, including *Obiter Dicta* (1884) and *Men,*

Women, and Books (1910), as well as a *Life of Charlotte Brontë* (1887). In this extract from that work, Birrell contrasts the raw vitality of *Jane Eyre* with what he believes to be the excessively refined novels of his own day.]

The crowning merit of *Jane Eyre* is its energy—a delightful quality at any time, but perhaps especially so just now. Some of our novelists make their characters walk through their parts after the languid fashions lately prevailing in the ball-room, and this proving irritating to some others of robuster frame of mind, has caused these latter, out of sheer temper, to make their heroines skip about like so many Kitty Clovers on the village green. But Jane Eyre neither languishes in drawing-rooms nor sits dangling her ankles upon gates, but is always interesting, eloquent, vehement. ⟨. . .⟩

Miss Brontë's errors lie on the surface, and can be easily removed. Half-a-dozen deletions and as many wisely-tempered alterations, and the work of correction would be done in any one of her novels. I am far from saying they would then be faultless, but at least they would be free from those faults which make the fortunes of small critics and jokes for the evening papers.

A novel like *Jane Eyre,* fresh from the hands of its creator—unmistakably alive—speaking a bold, unconventional language, recognizing love even in a woman's heart as something which does not always wait to be asked before springing into being, was sure to disturb those who worship the goddess Propriety. Prim women, living hardly on the interest of "a little hoard of maxims," men judiciously anxious to confine their own female folk to a diet of literary lentils, read *Jane Eyre* with undisguised alarm. There was an outrageous frankness about the book—a brushing away of phrases and formulas calculated to horrify those who, to do them justice, generally recognize an enemy when they see him.

—Augustine Birrell, *Life of Charlotte Brontë* (London: Walter Scott, 1887), pp. 105–8

VIRGINIA WOOLF ON CHARLOTTE BRONTË AS POET

[Virginia Woolf (1882–1941), aside from being one of the most distinguished British novelists of the twentieth century, was also an astute critic. Her critical work is gathered in several volumes, including *The Common Reader* (1925), *A Room of One's Own* (1929), and *The Moment and Other Essays* (1942). In this extract, Woolf finds *Jane Eyre* representative of a poetic instinct in Charlotte Brontë, in which the natural world symbolizes human emotions.]

Of the hundred years that have passed since Charlotte Brontë was born, she, the centre now of so much legend, devotion, and literature, lived but thirty-nine. It is strange to reflect how different those legends might have been had her life reached the ordinary human span. She might have become, like some of her famous contemporaries, a figure familiarly met with in London and elsewhere, the subject of pictures and anecdotes innumerable, the writer of many novels, of memoirs possibly, removed from us well within the memory of the middle-aged in all the splendour of established fame. She might have been wealthy, she might have been prosperous. But it is not so. When we think of her we have to imagine someone who had no lot in our modern world; we have to cast our minds back to the fifties of the last century, to a remote parsonage upon the wild Yorkshire moors. In that parsonage, and on those moors, unhappy and lonely, in her poverty and her exaltation, she remains for ever.

These circumstances, as they affected her character, may have left their traces on her work. A novelist, we reflect, is bound to build up his structure with much very perishable material which begins by lending it reality and ends by cumbering it with rubbish. As we open *Jane Eyre* once more we cannot stifle the suspicion that we shall find her world of imagination as antiquated, mid-Victorian, and out of date as the parsonage on the moor, a place only to be visited by the curious, only preserved by the pious. So we open *Jane Eyre;* and in two pages every doubt is swept clean from our minds.

> Folds of scarlet drapery shut in my view to the right hand; to the left were the clear panes of glass, protecting, but not separating me from the drear November day. At intervals, while turning over the leaves of my book, I studied the aspect of that winter afternoon. Afar, it offered a pale blank of mist and cloud; near, a scene of wet lawn and storm-beat shrub, with ceaseless rain sweeping away wildly before a long and lamentable blast.

There is nothing there more perishable than the moor itself, or more subject to the sway of fashion than the 'long and lamentable blast'. Nor is this exhilaration short-lived. It rushes us through the entire volume, without giving us time to think, without letting us lift our eyes from the page. So intense is our absorption that if someone moves in the room the movement seems to take place not there but up in Yorkshire. The writer has us by the hand, forces us along her road, makes us see what she sees, never leaves us for a moment or allows us to forget her. At the end we are steeped through and through with genius, the vehemence, the indignation of Charlotte Brontë. Remarkable faces, figures of strong outline and gnarled feature have flashed upon us in passing; but it is through her eyes that we have seen them. Once she is gone we seek for them in vain. Think of Rochester and we have to think of Jane Eyre. Think of the moor, and again there is Jane Eyre. Think of the drawing-room, even, those 'white carpets on which seemed laid brilliant garlands of flowers', that 'pale Parian mantelpiece' with its Bohemia glass of 'ruby red' and the 'general blending of snow and fire'—what is all that except Jane Eyre?

The drawbacks of being Jane Eyre are not far to seek. Always to be a governess and always to be in love is a serious limitation in a world which is full, after all, of people who are neither one nor the other. The characters of a Jane Austen or of a Tolstoy have a million facets compared with these. They live and are complex by means of their effect upon many different people who serve to mirror them in the round. They move hither and thither whether their creators watch them or not, and the world in which they live seems to us an independent world which we can visit, now that they have created it, by ourselves. Thomas Hardy is more akin to Charlotte Brontë in the power of his personality and the narrowness of his vision.

But the differences are vast. As we read *Jude the Obscure* we are not rushed to a finish; we brood and ponder and drift away from the text in plethoric trains of thought which build up round the characters an atmosphere of question and suggestion of which they are themselves, as often as not, unconscious. Simple peasants as they are, we are forced to confront them with destinies and questionings of the hugest import, so that often it seems as if the most important characters in a Hardy novel are those which have no names. Of this power, of this speculative curiosity, Charlotte Brontë has no trace. She does not attempt to solve the problems of human life; she is even unaware that such problems exist; all her force, and it is the more tremendous for being constricted, goes into the assertion, 'I love', 'I hate', 'I suffer'.

⟨. . .⟩ In other words, we read Charlotte Brontë not for exquisite observation of character—her characters are vigorous and elementary; not for comedy—hers is grim and crude; not for a philosophic view of life—hers is that of a country parson's daughter; but for her poetry. Probably that is so with all writers who have, as she has, an overpowering personality, so that, as we say in real life, they have only to open the door to make themselves felt. There is in them some untamed ferocity perpetually at war with the accepted order of things which makes them desire to create instantly rather than to observe patiently. This very ardour, rejecting half shades and other minor impediments, wing its way past the daily conduct of ordinary people and allies itself with their more inarticulate passions. It makes them poets, or, if they choose to write in prose, intolerant of its restrictions. Hence it is that both Emily and Charlotte are always invoking the help of nature. They both feel the need of some more powerful symbol of the vast and slumbering passions in human nature than words or actions can convey.
—Virginia Woolf, "*Jane Eyre* and *Wuthering Heights*" (1916), *Collected Essays,* ed. Leonard Woolf (New York: Harcourt, Brace & World, 1967), Vol. 1, pp. 185–88

[Richard Chase (1914–1962) wrote a number of critical works including *Herman Melville: A Critical Study* (1949). In this extract, Chase studies the emotional and social conflict between Jane Eyre and Rochester.]

In that somewhat fantastic Gothic-Byronic character Edward Rochester we have Charlotte Brontë's symbolic embodiment of the masculine *élan*. Jane Eyre's feelings toward Rochester are ambivalent. He draws her to him with a strange fascination; yet she is repelled by his animalism and his demonism. She wishes to submit herself to him; yet she cannot. She is nearly enthralled by the "tenderness and passion in every lineament" of his "kindled" face; yet she shrinks from the flashing of his "falcon eye" and from the glamor of his self-proclaimed guilt and his many exploits among women of other countries (in France, Céline; in Italy, Giacinta; in Germany, Clara—"these poor girls" Jane calls them). She cannot permit the proffered intimacies of this man who keeps a mad wife locked up in his attic. And if her moral scruples would allow his embrace, still she could not endure the intensity of his passion. The noble, free companionship of man and woman does not present itself to her as a possibility. She sees only two possible modes of behavior; meek submission or a flirtatious, gently sadistic skirmishing designed to keep her lover at bay. Finally her sense of "duty" compels Jane to run away. The inevitable parting of the lovers had been forecast when the lightning, summoned from the sky by their first declaration of love, had split the garden chestnut tree asunder.

The splitting of the tree, however, may also symbolize two alternate images of Jane Eyre's soul, two possible extremes which, as she believes, her behavior may take. At one extreme is Bertha, Rochester's mad wife; at the other is St. John Rivers, the clergyman cousin whom Jane meets after she flees Rochester and who wants to marry her. Before the story can end, Jane must purge these extreme images of herself. Bertha represents the women who has given herself blindly and uncompromisingly to the principle of sex and intellect. As

Fanny E. Ratchford (the expert in the voluminous juvenile romances written by the Brontës) has shown, the character of Bertha was evolved from a certain Lady Zenobia Ellrington, a heroine of Charlotte Brontë's childish fantasy-kingdom of Angria. Miss Ratchford describes Lady Zenobia thus: She was a "noble woman of strong mind and lofty thought. On the other hand, she is given to fits of rage in which she shrieks like a wild beast and falls upon her victim hand and foot. On one occasion she kicked Lord Charles [a juvenile version of Rochester] down the stairs." Always she is depicted as tall of stature and strong of body. Lord Charles once declared that she could spar on equal terms with her husband, "one of the best boxers on record." She was, furthermore, a learned and intellectual woman, a bluestocking in fact. Like Bertha, she was a Creole and came from a family notorious for mad crimes and passions. May not Bertha, Jane seems to ask herself, be a living example of what happens to the woman who gives herself to the Romantic Hero, who in her insane suffragettism tries herself to play the Hero, to be the fleshly vessel of the *élan*?

We may think that fear drives Jane away from Rochester; *she,* however, says that it is "duty." In St. John Rivers she meets duty incarnate. In a poem Charlotte Brontë had imagined herself as a missionary to the pagans. No "coward love of life," she says, has made "me shrink from the righteous strife." Rivers has given up Rosamond Oliver, a charming and life-loving girl, and wants to marry Jane and take her to India, where he plans to devote himself to missionary work. Plainly, it would be a sexless marriage. Rivers wants a wife to "influence." He is cold, selfish, fanatical—a narrow bigot, who shakes Jane's confidence in "duty." She cannot marry Rivers; she must purge her soul of the image of "duty" as she has of the image of Bertha.

How to resolve the plot? It must be done as Charlotte, the leader of her sisters in all practical matters, was accustomed to do things: by positive action. The universe conspiring against Jane Eyre, like the circumstances which so often conspired against the sisters, must be chastened by an assertion of will, catastrophic if necessary. And so Charlotte sends Rochester's house up in flames and makes him lose his eyesight and his left hand in a vain attempt to save Bertha. Rochester's injuries are, I should think, a symbolic castration. The faculty of vision, the analysts have shown, is often identified in the unconscious with the energy of sex. When Rochester had tried to make love to Jane, she felt a "fiery hand grasp at her vitals"; the hand, then, must be cut off. The universe, not previously amenable to supernatural communication between the parted lovers, now allows them to hear each other though they are leagues apart. It is as if the masterless universe had been subdued by being lopped, blinded, and burned. Jane Eyre now comes into her own. She returns to Rochester. She baits him coyly about her relations with Rivers; he exhibits manly jealousy. They settle down to a mild married life; they have a child; Rochester partly, but only partly, regains his eyesight. The tempo and energy of the universe can be quelled, we see, by a patient, practical woman.

—Richard Chase, "The Brontës, or, Myth Domesticated," *Forms of Modern Fiction*, ed. William Van O'Connor (Minneapolis: University of Minnesota Press, 1948), pp. 107–9

ROBERT B. HEILMAN ON CHARLOTTE BRONTË AND THE GOTHIC

[Robert B. Heilman (b. 1906), professor emeritus of English of the University of Washington, is a voluminous critic of literature and drama. Among his books are *Tragedy and Melodrama* (1968), *The Ghost on the Ramparts and Other Essays in the Humanities* (1973), and *The Southern Connection* (1991). In this extract, Heilman studies the way in which Brontë transformed the conventions of the Gothic novel into a form that can convey powerful emotion.]

From childhood terrors to all those mysteriously threatening sights, sounds, and injurious acts that reveal the presence of some malevolent force and that anticipate the holocaust at Thornfield, the traditional Gothic in *Jane Eyre* has often been noted, and as often disparaged. It need not be argued that

Charlotte Brontë did not reach the heights while using hand-me-down devices, though a tendency to work through the conventions of fictional art was a strong element in her make-up. This is true of all her novels, but it is no more true than her counter-tendency to modify, most interestingly, these conventions. In both *Villette* and *Jane Eyre* Gothic is used but characteristically is undercut.

Jane Eyre hears a "tragic . . . preternatural . . . laugh," but this is at "high noon" and there is "no circumstance of ghostliness"; Grace Poole, the supposed laugher, is a plain person, than whom no "apparition less romantic or less ghostly could . . . be conceived"; Charlotte apologizes ironically to the "romantic reader" for telling "the plain truth" that Grace generally bears a "pot of porter." Charlotte almost habitually revises "old Gothic," the relatively crude mechanisms of fear, with an infusion of the anti-Gothic. When Mrs. Rochester first tried to destroy Rochester by fire, Jane "baptized" Rochester's bed and heard Rochester "fulminating strange anathemas at finding himself lying in a pool of water." The introduction of comedy as a palliative of straight Gothic occurs on a large scale when almost seventy-five pages are given to the visit of the Ingram-Eshton party to mysterious Thornfield; here Charlotte, as often in her novels, falls into the manner of the Jane Austen whom she despised. When Mrs. Rochester breaks loose again and attacks Mason, the presence of guests lets Charlotte play the nocturnal alarum for at least a touch of comedy: Rochester orders the frantic women not to "pull me down or strangle me"; and "the two dowagers, in vast white wrappers, were bearing down on him like ships in full sail."

The symbolic also modifies the Gothic, for it demands of the reader a more mature and complicated response than the relatively simple thrill or momentary intensity of feeling sought by primitive Gothic. When mad Mrs. Rochester, seen only as "the foul German spectre—the Vampyre," spreads terror at night, that is one thing; when, with the malicious insight that is the paradox of her madness, she tears the wedding veil in two and thus symbolically destroys the planned marriage, that is another thing, far less elementary as art. The midnight blaze that ruins Thornfield becomes more than a shock when it is seen also as the fire of purgation; the grim, almost roadless forest surrounding Ferndean is more than a harrowing stage-set when it is also felt as a symbol of Rochester's closed-in life.

The point is that in various ways Charlotte manages to make the patently Gothic more than a stereotype. But more important is that she instinctively finds new ways to achieve the ends served by old Gothic—the discovery and release of new patterns of feeling, the intensification of feeling. Though only partly unconventional, Jane is nevertheless so portrayed as to evoke new feelings rather than merely exercise old ones. As a girl she is lonely, "passionate," "strange," "like nobody there"; she feels superior, rejects poverty, talks back precociously, tells truths bluntly, enjoys "the strangest sense of freedom," tastes "vengeance"; she experiences a nervous shock which is said to have a lifelong effect, and the doctor says "nerves not in a good state"; she can be "reckless and feverish," "bitter and truculent"; at Thornfield she is restless, given to "bright visions," letting "imagination" picture an existence full of "life, fire, feeling." Thus Charlotte leads away from standardized characterization toward new levels of human reality, and hence from stock responses toward a new kind of passionate engagement.

Charlotte moves toward depth in various ways that have an immediate impact like that of Gothic. Jane's strange, fearful symbolic dreams are not mere thrillers but reflect the tensions of the engagement period, the stress of the wedding-day debate with Rochester, and the longing for Rochester after she has left him. The final Thornfield dream, with its vivid image of a hand coming through a cloud in place of the expected moon, is in the surrealistic vein that appears most sharply in the extraordinary pictures that Jane draws at Thornfield: here Charlotte is plumbing the psyche, not inventing a weird *décor.* Likewise in the telepathy scene, which Charlotte, unlike Defoe in dealing with a similar episode, does her utmost to actualize: "The feeling was not like an electric shock; but it was quite as sharp, as strange, as startling: . . . that inward sensation . . . with all its unspeakable strangeness . . . like an inspiration . . . wondrous shock of feeling. . . ." In her flair for the surreal, in her plunging into feeling that is without status in the ordinary world of the novel, Charlotte discovers a new dimension of Gothic.

She does this most thoroughly in her portrayal of characters and of the relations between them. If in Rochester we see only an Angrian-Byronic hero and a Charlotte wish-fulfillment figure (the two identifications which to some readers seem entirely to place him), we miss what is more significant, the exploration of personality that opens up new areas of feeling in intersexual relationships. Beyond the "grim," the "harsh," the eccentric, the almost histrionically cynical that superficially distinguish Rochester from conventional heroes, there is something almost Lawrentian: Rochester is "neither tall nor graceful"; his eyes can be "dark, irate, and piercing"; his strong features "took my feelings from my own power and fettered them in his." Without using the vocabulary common to us, Charlotte is presenting maleness and physicality, to which Jane responds directly. She is "assimilated" to him by "something in my brain and heart, in my blood and nerves"; she "must love" and "could not unlove" him; the thought of parting from him is "agony." Rochester's oblique amatory maneuvers become almost punitive in the Walter-to-Griselda style and once reduce her to sobbing "convulsively"; at times the love-game borders on a power-game. Jane, who prefers "rudeness" to "flattery," is an instinctive evoker of passion: she learns "the pleasure of vexing and soothing him by turns" and pursues a "system" of working him up "to considerable irritation" and coolly leaving him; when, as a result, his caresses become grimaces, pinches, and tweaks, she records that, sometimes at least, she "decidedly preferred these fierce favors." She reports, "I crushed his hand . . . red with the passionate pressure"; she "could not . . . see God for his creature," and in her devotion Rochester senses "an earnest, religious energy."

Charlotte's remolding of stock feeling reaches a height when she sympathetically portrays Rochester's efforts to make Jane his mistress; here the stereotyped seducer becomes a kind of lost nobleman of passion, and of specifically physical passion: "Every atom of your flesh is as dear to me as my own. . . ." The intensity of the pressure which he puts upon her is matched, not by the fear and revulsion of the popular heroine, but by a responsiveness which she barely masters: "The crisis was perilous; but not without its charm . . ." She is "tortured by a sense of remorse at thus hurting his feelings"; at the moment of decision "a hand of fiery iron grasped my vitals . . . blackness, burning! . . . my intolerable duty"; she leaves in "despair"; and after she has left, "I longed to be his; I panted to return . . ."— and for the victory of principle "I abhorred myself . . . I was hateful in my own eyes." This extraordinary openness to feeling, this escape from the bondage of the trite, continues in the Rivers relationship, which is a structural parallel to the Rochester affair: as in Rochester the old sex villain is seen in a new perspective, so in Rivers the clerical hero is radically refashioned; and Jane's almost accepting a would-be husband is given the aesthetic status of a regrettable yielding to a seducer. Without a remarkable liberation from conventional feeling Charlotte could not fathom the complexity of Rivers— the earnest and dutiful clergyman distraught by a profound inner turmoil of conflicting "drives": sexuality, restlessness, hardness, pride, ambition ("fever in his vitals," "inexorable as death"); the hypnotic, almost inhuman potency of his influence on Jane, who feels "a freezing spell," "an awful charm," an "iron shroud"; the relentlessness, almost the unscrupulousness, of his wooing, the resultant fierce struggle (like that with Rochester), Jane's brilliantly perceptive accusation, ". . . you almost hate me . . . you would kill me. You are killing me now"; and yet her mysterious near-surrender: "I was tempted to cease struggling with him—to rush down the torrent of his will into the gulf of his existence, and there lose my own."

Aside from partial sterilization of banal Gothic by dry factuality and humor, Charlotte goes on to make a much more important—indeed, a radical—revision of the mode: in *Jane Eyre* and in the other novels, as we shall see, that discovery of passion, that rehabilitation of the extra-rational, which is the historical office of Gothic, is no longer oriented in marvelous circumstance but moves deeply into the lesser known realities of human life. This change I describe as the change from "old Gothic" to "new Gothic." The kind of appeal is the same; the fictional method is utterly different.

—Robert B. Heilman, "Charlotte Brontë's 'New' Gothic," *From Jane Austen to Joseph Conrad,* ed. Robert C. Rathburn and Martin Steinmann, jr. (Minneapolis: University of Minnesota Press, 1958), pp. 120–23

ROBERT BERNARD MARTIN ON THE COSMIC SCOPE OF BRONTË'S IMAGINATION

[Robert Bernard Martin (b. 1918) is Citizens' Professor of Humanities at the University of Hawaii. He has written biographies of Tennyson (1980), Edward FitzGerald (1985), and Gerard Manley Hopkins (1991). In this extract from his book on Charlotte Brontë's novels, Martin finds the greatness of *Jane Eyre* to rest in the cosmic scope of Brontë's imagination, which takes all of life for its focus.]

'Novelists should never allow themselves to weary of the study of real life,' wrote Charlotte Brontë with sweet reasonableness in *The Professor.* Then, rather less convincingly: 'If they observed this duty conscientiously, they would give us fewer pictures chequered with vivid contrasts of light and shade; they would seldom elevate their heroes and heroines to the heights of rapture—still seldomer sink them to the depths of despair; for if we rarely taste the fulness of joy in this life, we yet more rarely savour the acrid bitterness of hopeless anguish.' In short, such conscientious novelists would not write *Jane Eyre.*

The primary impression of Miss Brontë's first masterpiece is of anguished torment and nearly intolerable happiness. Because she believed that life's joys are few beside its sorrows, ⟨. . .⟩ the reader's strongest recollection is probably of the blinding fierceness of the rebellion of Jane's lonely heart against the loveless tyranny of Gateshead, the pangs of her physical and emotional hunger at Lowood, the aching frustration of her first love of Rochester, the death-in-life of her discovery that he is already married, the solitary agony of her night on the moor, her merciless grinding under the juggernaut of St. John's ambitious piety. The fitful ecstasy of Jane's joy is made brighter by being thrown in relief against her trials and by the rareness of its visitation: the lyrical garden scene when Rochester pours out his love against a counterpoint of the nightingale's song; the night when he swoops her into his saddle before him like a demon lover enveloping her in his cloak; the muted, autumnal delicacy of their reconciliation at Ferndean, poised between laughter and tears.

The play of Charlotte Brontë's imagination achieves many of its finest effects by lurid contrasts of illumination and shade, by the relentless light of rational day set against the menacing shadows of dead of night ('ever the hour of fatality at Thornfield'), by the juxtaposition of pinafores and supernatural flashes of light, burnt porridge and raging epidemic, schoolroom doldrums and the long, terrible laughter of Grace Poole—or is it the lunatic mirth of Bertha?—housecleaning and a universe shaken by supernatural convulsions: the counterpoise of a world of mundane detail and the world of Gothic imagination. It is a witch's broth of ingredients, but for the first time Charlotte Brontë has the imaginative, comprehensive grasp of her material that manages to fuse its disparate parts into a real unity, one probably owing more to the singleness of her vision than it does to her formal considerations of the problems of structure in the novel. Whether the pattern she achieved was a completely deliberate and rational one, or whether it sprang from somewhere beneath the surface of her consciousness is ultimately unimportant. The heart has its forms, as well as its reasons, that the reason knows nothing of. The novel is improbable in the sense that all cosmic and supernatural action is improbable, even when it seems inevitable. It is larger than life because it is Miss Brontë's vision of the totality of life, of man's relation to his heart, mind, loved ones, and God, and any such vision must necessarily transcend the probable limits of experience of any individual.

—Robert Bernard Martin, *"Jane Eyre," The Accents of Persuasion: Charlotte Brontë's Novels* (New York: Norton, 1966), pp. 57–58

RICHARD BENVENUTO ON JANE EYRE'S MORAL CHOICES

[Richard Benvenuto is the author of *Emily Brontë* (1982) and *Amy Lowell* (1985). In this extract, Benvenuto asserts that the chief conflict in *Jane Eyre* is in Jane's moral struggle between the state of nature and the state of grace.]

If Jane's conflict had as its base a single personality, the conflict would be resolvable once Jane learned to adjust the relative claims of her reason and her emotions upon her sense of self-identity, and once she learned to use either as a corrective for the exaggerated claims of the other. But nature and grace do not make relative claims upon Jane. They stand for two self-identities, for forces inclusive of her whole being, which is divided so completely that two self-images claim possession of all her human faculties. When Jane defends the moral integrity of the poor, she is not speaking passionately and in defiance of reason, or vice versa. She is emotionally, intellectually, and morally convinced of what she says. And likewise, with her total being, reflectively and feelingly, she revolts from the memory of having had to beg. Not one unitive personality with different parts to it, but two unitive personalities contesting against each other make up her character. There is much to be said for seeing her conflict as critics have generally presented it—not the least of which is that it results in a novel of greater consistency than I am able to find. The portraits of Rochester and St. John speak more directly to a conflict between passion and conscience than perhaps they do to the larger division of nature and grace. But even if it turns out that Rochester and St. John are no more than embodiments of passion and conscience, they cause Jane to define her total being in two ways, to commit herself to two schemes of existence, in each of which there is room for different notions of passionate and rational behavior. A character divided by passion and conscience normally will fluctuate between them as he comes under the temporary sway of each. Though she contradicts herself, Jane does not fluctuate, properly speaking. She makes firm commitments to the life offered by nature and to the life offered by grace.

Jane's commitment to nature occurs when she hears Rochester's voice, just as St. John is about to coerce her into accepting an empty form of marriage. It is a complete endorsement of her own personality, a recognition of her native self as its own absolute norm. Rochester's voice was "no miracle," but the "work of nature. She was roused, and did . . . her best."

Nature, in this role, is not an impersonal force or an abstract, external system. The next morning Jane remembers a strange "inward sensation" preceding Rochester's voice. The voice itself had "seemed in *me*—not in the external world." It was "like an inspiration. The wondrous shock of feeling had come like the earthquake which shook the foundations of Paul and Silas's prison; it had opened the doors of the soul's cell and loosed its bands" (original italics). St. John represents duty, suppression, obedience: the behavior and the attitude required by the absolute external morality of grace. He would force Jane to seek acceptance in the terms of the law he serves, with no more room for compromise than he has given himself. These is no meeting the demands of grace halfway. Jane must either go to India as St. John's lawful wife, or not go at all. As Jane's description of it makes clear, Rochester's voice is her voice speaking in the tones of an absolute internal norm—nature, or her individuality. The voice reveals to her the foundations of her being. It is a power like an earthquake, breaking down the prison of religious duty and social code. It is as fundamental as breathing—an inspiration. As her liberation from the false ascendency of St. John, Rochester's voice speaks for Jane's truest life, not merely for her feelings, but for her deepest aspirations, her self-consciousness. There can be no mistake about the intent of the episode. Jane is right to assume the ascendency over St. John, right to leave him, and right to speak for her individual self and unique portion of existence.

But though it is clear that Jane is right to commit herself totally to nature, when St. John would force her into the service of grace, it is not clear how this commitment affects or even relates to her earlier, equally entire commitment to grace, when Rochester asks her to align herself with nature and become his mistress. Jane's return to Rochester raises the question of why she left him, though Jane never acknowledges that it was an error to have left him. Charlotte Brontë does not mean it to appear as such. She sanctions Jane's leaving St. John to return to Rochester, and she sanctions Jane's leaving Rochester and taking the road that leads her to St. John. Jane herself senses that her directions are unclear, but she can express her predicament only through the abstractions, judgment and principle. Just before she hears Rochester's voice,

Jane says that she "was almost as hard beset" now as she "had been once before, in a different way, by another. I was a fool both times. To have yielded then would have been an error of principle; to have yielded now would have been an error of judgment." She might have said, almost a fool, since she did not yield to either. Jane's assessment of her dilemma, however, is a more comprehensive one than would be required by a conflict limited to conscience and passion. It is as close as Jane comes to recognizing the totality of the commitments exacted by nature and grace.

The choice between the two amounts to a choice between a relativistic or situational morality and a fixed, universal moral code, between living outside any established religious framework and living as a Christian. Speaking for Christianity and for a moral code handed down through time, St. John asks Jane to continue in the direction she took when she left Rochester, the direction of principle or moral law not subject to individual variation or change. To have yielded would have been an error of judgment, a violation of the thought and moral awareness which she brings to her time. Rochester, on the other hand, makes an explicit appeal to a relativistic ethics and to Jane's innate powers of thought and her right to a self-made moral life. "Is it better," Rochester asks, "to drive a fellow-creature to despair than to transgress a mere human law—no man being injured by the breach?" The "mere human law" is the commandment forbidding adultery and the cultural ban on bigamy. To have yielded would have been an error of principle, against Jane's sense of what is everywhere and eternally right. To put Jane's statement somewhat differently: by opposing Rochester, she yielded to a sense of her moral life as properly under the control and guidance of others, authorities with greater responsibility than her own; by opposing St. John, she yielded to a sense of her moral life as properly under her control and shaping, and she accepts the responsibility for self-guidance. As she leaves one man and then the other, she travels the two existences of the child of grace and the child of nature.

—Richard Benvenuto, "The Child of Nature, the Child of Grace, and the Unresolved Conflict of *Jane Eyre*," *ELH* 39, No. 4 (December 1972): 631–33

[Nina Auerbach (b. 1943), a professor of English at the University of Pennsylvania, is one of the leading feminist critics of our time. Among her books are *Communities of Women* (1978), *Romantic Imprisonment* (1985), and *Private Theatricals: The Lives of the Victorians* (1990). In this extract, Auerbach finds that Rochester and his residence of Thornfield are reflections of Jane Eyre's emotional state.]

Thornfield and Rochester are from the beginning a reflection of Jane's inner world. She applies for the position only after Miss Temple has left Lowood, when she feels in herself 'the stirring of old emotions' which had, presumably, been frozen over by Lowood and subdued by Miss Temple. At Thornfield, the fairy-tales of her childhood, associated especially with the red room, seem to come to life: the drawing room seems 'a fairy place,' she approaches Bertha's quarters and thinks prophetically of 'a corridor in some Bluebeard's castle,' she hears Rochester's horse and thinks of 'Bessie's Gytrash.' Jane alone can speak French to Adèle, a language which had ambiguous underground connotations for Charlotte Brontë: she may have associated it with the sudden conflagration of emotion brought about in Brussels by M. Héger, to whom she spoke and wrote only in French. Bertha puts on Jane's wedding veil and looks in her mirror: in the red room, Jane had seen herself in the mirror as 'half fairy, half imp,' and now Bertha's reflection reminds her of 'the foul German spectre—the Vampyre.' Adèle, the sensual child, and Bertha, whose uncontrolled passion has run into insanity, come from Jane's own fire, just as Helen Burns and Miss Temple came from her ice. Thornfield embodies the attraction and the danger of the desires that arise when Miss Temple's restraint is withdrawn; just before Jane flees Rochester's anarchic love for her, she dreams that she is lying once again in the red room at Gateshead.

Away from Thornfield, the world is again obdurate and hostile. Jane arrives in a town that is 'no town . . . but a stone pillar.' The 'sympathies of Nature with man' are withdrawn, though at first she expects still to be cherished by the 'universal mother, Nature':

I touched the heath: it was dry, and yet warm with the heat of the summer day. I looked at the sky; it was pure: a kindly star twinkled just above the chasm ridge. The dew fell, but with propitious softness; no breeze whispered. Nature *seemed to me* benign and good; I *thought* she loved me, outcast as I was; and I, who from man could anticipate only mistrust, rejection, insult, clung to her with filial fondness. Tonight, at least, I would be her guest—as I was her child: my mother would lodge me without money and without price. [My italics]

But on the next night, the sentimental hope that lingers from Thornfield is dispelled by the return of the hostile nature of Lowood and Gateshead: 'my night was wretched, my rest broken: the ground was damp, the air cold; besides, intruders had passed near me more than once, and I had again and again to change my quarters: no sense of safety or tranquillity befriended me. Towards morning it rained; the whole of the following day was wet.' At Moor House, she will refer to nature as a 'stinted stepmother.'

St John Rivers is the emotional alternative to Rochester in a world that seems to generate only extremes of fire and ice. The snow-ice-stone imagery that surrounds him, and his severe Christianity, recall the world of Lowood, Mr Brocklehurst, and hell in-burns. The parallel family structure, two sisters and a brother, even look back to the unyielding Reeds at Gateshead and their 'death-white' landscape. Improbably as Charlotte Brontë handles the incident, it is important to the novel that St John is Jane's cousin, and that Moor House is as close as she comes to arriving at her origins, the home she has inherited. His ice is in Jane as well. When her buried emotions began to stir, Thornfield rose up embodying them; when she forces down her passion in the name of Christian principle, she meets her icy cousin, who is forcing down *his* passion for Rosamond Oliver in order to fulfil his spiritual mission. Even his name, St John, suggests Jane's own potential sanctification. If nature was aroused by Rochester's proposal, Heaven is aroused by St John's: 'All was changing utterly, with a sudden sweep. Religion called—Angels beckoned—God commanded—life rolled together like a scroll—death's gates opening, showed eternity beyond: it seemed, that for safety and bliss there, all here might be sacrificed in a second.' The apocalyptic imagery underlines the fact that the governess Jane always had the potential of becoming a Blakean angel.

Jane's marriage to Rochester at Ferndean and her final home there seem less a synthesis of the two worlds than a partial conquest of one world by the other. The fire of Thornfield is extinguished with Rochester's 'flaming and flashing eyes,' and replaced by motifs from the Lowood-Moor House world: Rochester is 'stone blind,' a 'sightless block,' and Bertha, the source of the fire, is now 'dead as the stones on which her brains and blood were scattered.' Like Lowood, Ferndean is built on an "ineligible and insalubrious site': nature no longer nurtures the self, but is somewhat threatening and tainted. Rochester's unlikely conversion to orthodox Christianity suggests the triumph of the Calvinist God, who has been an anti-life force throughout the novel, over the pagan pantheon of Thornfield: there are 'no flowers, no garden-beds' at Ferndean; it is 'as still as a church on a week-day.' The book does not end with Rochester's love lyrics, but with St John's self-immolating cry to this implacable and unnatural divinity. Despite the apparent victory of Jane's fire over St John's ice, of her 'powers' over his God, his country and Mr Brocklehurst's seem to have triumphed after all. Everything that Rochester represented was crushed with Thornfield, and our final sense of the book is that 'reality' is 'imagination,' broken and blind. Jane, who would not be Rochester's mistress, becomes his governess, and the triumph of this side of her character sends us forward to Lucy Snowe, in whose nature 'the world below' is a more imperious force, requiring an even greater distortion of nature to suppress it.

—Nina Auerbach, "Charlotte Brontë: The Two Countries," *University of Toronto Quarterly* 42, No. 4 (Summer 1973): 333–35

ADRIENNE RICH ON JANE EYRE AND BERTHA ROCHESTER

[Adrienne Rich (b. 1929), a prolific American poet, is also a leading feminist and critic. Among her critical works are *Of Woman Born: Motherhood as Experience and Institution* (1976) and *Compulsory Heterosexuality and Lesbian Experience* (1981). In this extract, Rich asserts that Bertha Rochester, the mad wife of Edward Rochester, is a symbol of what Jane Eyre might become in the patriarchal world of Victorian England.]

It is interesting that the Thornfield episode is often recalled or referred to as if it *were* the novel *Jane Eyre*. So truncated and abridged, that novel would become the following: A young woman arrives as governess at a large country house inhabited by a small French girl and an older housekeeper. She is told that the child is the ward of the master of the house, who is traveling abroad. Presently the master comes home and the governess falls in love with him, and he with her. Several mysterious and violent incidents occur in the house which seem to center around one of the servants, and which the master tells the governess will all be explained once they are married. On the wedding day, it is revealed that he has a wife still alive, a madwoman who is kept under guard in the upper part of the house and who is the source of the sinister incidents. The governess decides that her only course of action is to leave her lover forever. She steals away from the house and settles in another part of the country. After some time she returns to the manor house to find it has burned to the ground, the madwoman is dead, and her lover, though blinded and maimed by the fire, is free to marry her.

Thus described, the novel becomes a blend of Gothic horror and Victorian morality. That novel might have been written by many a contributor to ladies' magazines, but it is not the novel written by Charlotte Brontë. If the Thornfield episode is central, it is because in it Jane comes to womanhood and to certain definitive choices about what it means to her to be a woman. There are three aspects of this episode: the house, Thornfield itself; Mr. Rochester, the Man; and the madwoman, Jane's alter ego.

Charlotte Brontë gives us an extremely detailed and poetically convincing vision of Thornfield. Jane reaches its door by darkness, after a long journey; she scarcely knows what the house is like till the next day when Mrs. Fairfax, the housekeeper, takes her through it on a tour which ends in the upper regions, on the rooftop. The reader's sense of its luxury, its isolation, and its mysteries is precisely Jane's, seen with the eyes of a young woman just come from the dormitory of a charity school—a young woman of strong sensuality. But it is the upper regions of the house which are of crucial importance— the part of the house Jane lives in least, yet which most affects her life. Here she first hears that laugh—"distinct, formal, mirthless"—which is ascribed to the servant Grace Poole and which she will later hear outside her own bedroom door. Here, too, standing on the roof, or walking up and down in the corridor, close to the very door behind which the madwoman is kept hidden, she gives silent vent to those feelings which are introduced by the telling phrase: "Anybody may blame me who likes . . ."

The phrase introduces a passage which is Charlotte Brontë's feminist manifesto. Written one hundred and twenty-six years ago, it is still having to be written over and over today, in different language but with essentially the same sense that sentiments of this kind are still unacceptable to many, and that in uttering them one lays oneself open to blame and to entrenched resistance:

> It is in vain to say human beings ought to be satisfied with tranquility: they must have action; and they will make it if they cannot find it. Millions are condemned to a stiller doom than mine, and millions are in silent revolt against their lot. Nobody knows how many rebellions besides political rebellions ferment in the masses of life which people earth. Women are supposed to be very calm generally; but women feel just as men feel; they need exercise for their faculties, and a field for their efforts as much as their brothers do; they suffer from too rigid a restraint, too absolute a stagnation, precisely as men would suffer; and it is narrow-minded in their more privileged fellow-creatures to say that they ought to confine themselves to making puddings and knitting stockings, to playing on the piano and embroidering bags. It is thoughtless to condemn them, or laugh at them, if they seek to do more or learn more than custom has pronounced necessary for their sex.

Immediately thereafter we are made to hear again the laugh of the madwoman. I want to remind you of another mad wife who appears in a novel of our own time—the woman Lynda in

Doris Lessing's *The Four-Gated City,* who inhabits not the upper story but the cellar, and with whom the heroine Martha (like Jane Eyre an employee and in love with her employer) finally goes to live, experiencing her madness with her.

For Jane Eyre, the upper regions are not what Gaston Bachelard calls in the *The Poetics of Space* "the rationality of the roof" as opposed to the unconscious and haunted world of the cellar. Or, the roof is where Jane is visited by an expanding vision, but this vision, this illumination, brings her close to the madwoman captive behind the door. In Lessing's novel the madwoman is herself a source of illumination. Jane has no such contact with Bertha Rochester. Yet Jane's sense of herself as a woman—as equal to and with the same needs as a man—is next-door to insanity in England in the 1840s. Jane never feels herself to be going mad, but there is a madwoman in the house who exists as her opposite, her image horribly distorted in a warped mirror, a threat to her happiness. Just as her instinct for self-preservation saves her from earlier temptations, so it must save her from becoming this woman by curbing her imagination at the limits of what is bearable for a powerless woman in the England of the 1840s.

—Adrienne Rich, "Jane Eyre: The Temptations of a Motherless Woman" (1973), *On Lies, Secrets, and Silence: Selected Prose 1966–1978* (New York: Norton, 1979), pp. 96–99

TERRY EAGLETON ON JANE EYRE'S AUTONOMY

[Terry Eagleton (b. 1943), a fellow of Wadham College, Oxford, is a distinguished British literary critic who has specialized in the analysis of literature from a sociopolitical perspective of a sort often associated with Marxist criticism. Among his many books are *Criticism and Ideology* (1976), *Literary Theory: An Introduction* (1983), and *William Shakespeare* (1986). In this extract from his Marxist study of the Brontës, Eagleton maintains that Jane Eyre is representative of a long line of Brontë characters who remain free from personal bonds and retain autonomy.]

At the centre of all Charlotte's novels, I am arguing, is a figure who either lacks or deliberately cuts the bonds of kinship. This leaves the self a free, blank, 'pre-social' atom: free to be injured and exploited, but free also to progress, move through the class-structure, choose and forge relationships, strenuously utilise its talents in scorn of autocracy or paternalism. The novels are deeply informed by this bourgeois ethic, but there is more to be said than that. For the social status finally achieved by the *déraciné* self is at once meritoriously won and inherently proper. Jane's uncle is said to be a tradesman, and the Reeds despise her for it; but Bessie comments that the Eyres were as much gentry as the Reeds, and her Rivers cousins have an impressively ancient lineage. Rochester seems a grander form of gentry, and Jane's relationship with him is of course socially unequal; but it is, nevertheless, a kind of returning home as well as an enviable move upwards. Given relationships are certainly constrictive: they mediate a suave violence deep-seated in society itself, as John Reed's precociously snobbish remark suggests. But knowing where you genetically belong still counts for a good deal in the end. Charlotte's fiction portrays the unprotected self in its lonely conquest of harsh conditions, and so intimates a meritocratic vision; but individualist self-reliance leads you to roles and relations which are objectively fitting.

Jane, then, disowns what second-hand kin she has, caring never to see the Reeds again, surviving instead by her own talents; she creates the relationships which matter, those of spiritual rather than blood affinity. ('I believe [Rochester] is of mine;—I am sure he is,—I feel akin to him . . . though rank and wealth sever us widely, I have something in my brain and heart, in my blood and nerves, that assimilates me mentally to him.') Spiritual affinity, indeed, is more physical and full-blooded than the icy *rapport* one has with literal kinsfolk like Rivers. In this as in other ways, however, Jane is granted the best of both worlds. Just as her resources for solitary survival run out, on the long exhausting flight from Thornfield, she is supplied with a new set of kinsfolk who turn out this time to be pleasant. The Rivers sisters provide a cultivated retreat into which Jane can temporarily relax; she rests her head on Diana's lap in delighted gratitude at her discovery of blood-relations, even though the event will prove merely a stopping-off place *en route* to the grander gentility of Rochester. This time, however, her relation to kinsfolk is not that of servile dependence. On the contrary, it is they who are now in part dependent on her: each of them gets a quarter share of her new-found wealth. The legacy allows Jane to combine sturdy independence with a material sealing of her affinity with others. Given relationships are good, if you may negotiate them on your own terms; kinsmen are both gift and threat. It is an ambivalence reflected in Jane's feelings towards Mrs Reed: she upbraids her hotly for neglecting familial duty, but curiously excuses that brutality by wondering 'how could she really like an interloper not of her race, and unconnected with her, after her husband's death, by any tie?' Whether 'race' matters or not seems a moot point in Jane's own mind.

Jane's relative isolation from given relationships results in a proud autonomy of spirit, one which in some ways implicitly questions the class-structure. She has too much self-respect to lavish her love on an unresponsive Rochester: 'He is not of your order; keep to your caste; and be too self-respecting to lavish the love of the whole heart, soul, and strength, where such a gift is not wanted and may be despised.' Yet the comment, of course, endorses the class-structure as well as suggesting the spiritual inferiority of one's betters: if the callously insensitive aristocrat cannot recognise a gift when he sees one, then it is wise to remain self-righteously on one's own side of the social divide. In so far as it is for him to make the overture, Jane's attitude combines deference with independence; yet 'independence' is a thoroughly ambiguous term. It means not wanting to be a servant, which implies a class-judgement on those below you as well as suggesting a radical attitude to those above. Jane's rebellion against the Reeds engages certain egalitarian feelings: she rejects the idea of paternalist benefaction as disagreeable, and later values her equal relationship with Mrs Fairfax for the freedom it brings. 'The equality between her and me was real; not the mere result of condescension on her part; so much the better—my position was all the freer.' But independence in this society involves attaining a precarious gentility (Bessie has to admit that the adult Jane is now, at least, a lady), and that in turn entails a sharp eye for the nuance of social distinction. Jane is furious with the Reeds because they treat her as a servant when she isn't one; her smouldering hatred of their snobbery is thus shot through with shared class-assumptions about the poor. ('No; I should not like to belong to poor people.') Her response to the pupils at Morton school is similarly double-edged: distasteful though she finds their unmannerliness, she 'must not forget that these coarsely-clad little peasants are of flesh and blood as good as the scions of the gentlest genealogy; and that the germs of native excellence, refinement, intelligence, kind feeling, are as likely to exist in their hearts as in those of the best born.' The demotic generosity of this is sharply qualified by that stern self-reminder; Jane's doctrine of spiritual equality stems logically from her own experience, but it has to fight hard against the social discriminations bred into an expensively clad child. (Her egalitarian defence of the 'British peasantry' is based, ironically, on a dogma of chauvinist superiority: they are at least preferable to their 'ignorant, coarse, and besotted' European counterparts.) Jane feels degraded by her role as schoolmistress ('I had taken a step which sank instead of raising me in the scale of social existence'), but guiltily scorns the feeling as 'idiotic'; and that tension deftly defines the petty-bourgeois consciousness which clings to real class-distinctions while spiritually rejecting them. She is, for instance, priggishly quick to point out to the Rivers' servant Hannah that she may be a beggar but at least she is a high-class one:

> 'Are you book-learned?' [Hannah] inquired, presently.
> 'Yes, very.'

The snobbish Hannah must be given an object-lesson in social equality, taught not to judge by appearances, so Jane reveals how superior she is to the old woman. Even in beggary class counts: St John Rivers, presumably noting Jane's refined accent when Hannah turns her from his door, surmises instantly that this is a 'peculiar case'. Jane's insistence on getting past the servant and appealing to the young ladies glimpsed within is, indeed, sound class tactics: the sisters are presented as idealised versions of herself, quiet, spiritual and self-composed.

—Terry Eagleton, *Myths of Power: A Marxist Study of the Brontës* (London: Macmillan, 1975), pp. 26–29

NANCY PELL ON *JANE EYRE* AND HISTORY

[Nancy Pell is an American literary critic who, in the following extract, studies the historical focus of *Jane Eyre*. Pell declares that the references to historical revolutions are symbolic of Jane Eyre's own emotional state.]

Two allusions in the novel to actual rebellions in English history suggest Charlotte Brontë's awareness that Jane's struggle for a wider life has significant historical implications. First, after a lesson at Lowood school on tonnage and poundage in the early reign of Charles I, Helen Burns confesses her admiration for the Stuart king.

> "I was wondering how a man who wished to do right could act so unjustly and unwisely as Charles the First sometimes did . . . what a pity it was that, with his integrity and conscientiousness, he could see no farther than the prerogatives of the crown. . . . Still, I like Charles—I respect him—I pity him, poor, murdered king! Yes, his enemies were the worst: they shed blood they had no right to shed. How dared they kill him!"

Jane criticizes Helen, both for her visionary passivity and for her royalist sympathies. "If people were always kind and obedient to those who are cruel and unjust," Jane objects, "the wicked people would have it all their own way: they would never feel afraid, and so they would never alter, but would grow worse and worse." Her resistance to the abuse of power, even the Stuart prerogatives, here clearly places Jane among the regicides. Helen tells her that the theory of retribution she has just described is held only by heathens and savage tribes, but Jane's experience dismisses Helen's received doctrine. To her, loving one's enemies means that "I should love Mrs. Reed, which I cannot do; I should bless her son John, which is impossible." Eventually Jane comes to comprehend the value of self-restraint through the example of Miss Temple, director of Lowood, whose quiet resistance to Mr. Brocklehurst's policies of deprivation has nothing to do with axiomatic stoicism. Jane modifies Helen's quietism with Miss Temple's nurturing concern for body and mind and emerges from her childhood, as Q. D. Leavis points out, with an appreciation for self-discipline as a strategy of psychological warfare.

The second reference to historical revolutionary antecedents is both more subtle and more powerful in its implications. Early in the novel the servant Abbot suspects that young Jane is "a sort of infantine Guy Fawkes"; the passage is echoed later on when Jane has become a school mistress in the village of Morton. She receives a visit from St. John on the occasion of a holiday from her duties on the fifth of November. Although the day is not named, it is the traditional British Guy Fawkes Day. The date is not without ambiguities however. In addition to marking the discovery of the Catholic plot to blow up the Houses of Parliament in 1605, it is also the anniversary of the landing of William and Mary at Torbay in the "Glorious Revolution" of 1688. Thus both violent and bloodless rebellions are juxtaposed on the occasion of Jane's passing from the dispossessed to the possessing class. For during his brief visit, St. John—who knows Jane only as Jane Elliott—looks at a sketch that she has drawn and discovers her true name, Jane Eyre, written on the portrait cover. This disclosure leads to the rediscovery of lost connections between Jane and the Rivers family and establishes her possession of the legacy of twenty thousand pounds from her uncle John Eyre. The repeated image of Guy Fawkes and the ambiguous historical allusions to the Fifth of November thus accompany the moment that unites Jane's past and her future.

—Nancy Pell, "Resistance, Rebellion, and Marriage: The Economics of *Jane Eyre*," *Nineteenth-Century Fiction* 31, No. 4 (March 1977): 405–7

SANDRA M. GILBERT AND SUSAN GUBAR ON THE OPENING OF
JANE EYRE

[Sandra M. Gilbert (b. 1936), a professor of English at
the University of California at Davis, and Susan Gubar
(b. 1944), a professor of English at Indiana University,
wrote a history of women's writing in the nineteenth
century, *The Madwoman in the Attic* (1979), followed
by a three-volume study of women's writing in this
century, *No Man's Land* (1988–94). In this extract from
the earlier volume, Gilbert and Gubar study the opening of *Jane Eyre,* which they find representative of the
emotional conflicts throughout the novel.]

Unlike many Victorian novels, which begin with elaborate
expository paragraphs, *Jane Eyre* begins with a casual, curiously
enigmatic remark: "There was no possibility of taking a walk
that day." Both the occasion ("that day") and the excursion (or
the impossibility of one) are significant: the first is the real
beginning of Jane's pilgrim's progress toward maturity; the
second is a metaphor for the problems she must solve in order
to attain maturity. "I was glad" not to be able to leave the
house, the narrator continues: "dreadful to me was the coming
home in the raw twilight . . . humbled by the consciousness of
my physical inferiority" (chap. 1). As many critics have com-
mented, Charlotte Brontë consistently uses the opposed properties of fire and ice to characterize Jane's experiences, and her
technique is immediately evident in these opening passages.
For while the world outside Gateshead is almost unbearably
wintry, the world within is claustrophobic, fiery, like ten-year-
old Jane's own mind. Excluded from the Reed family group in
the drawing room because *she* is not a "contented, happy, little child"—excluded, that is, from "normal" society—Jane takes
refuge in a scarlet-draped window seat where she alternately
stares out at the "drear November day" and reads of polar
regions in Bewick's *History of British Birds.* The "death-white
realms" of the Arctic fascinate her; she broods upon "the multi-
plied rigors of extreme cold" as if brooding upon her own
dilemma: whether to stay in, behind the oppressively scarlet
curtain, or to go out into the cold of a loveless world.

Her decision is made for her. She is found by John Reed, the tyrannical son of the family, who reminds her of her anomalous position in the household, hurls the heavy volume of Bewick at her, and arouses her passionate rage. Like a "rat," a "bad animal," a "mad cat," she compares him to "Nero, Caligula, etc." and is borne away to the red-room, to be imprisoned literally as well as figuratively. For "the fact is," confesses the grownup narrator ironically, "I was [at that moment] a trifle beside myself; or rather *out* of myself, as the French would say. . . . like any other rebel slave, I felt resolved . . . to go all lengths" (chap. 1).

But if Jane was "out of" herself in her struggle against John Reed, her experience in the red-room, probably the most metaphorically vibrant of all her early experiences, forces her deeply into herself. For the red-room, stately, chilly, swathed in rich crimson, with a great white bed and an easy chair "like a pale throne" looming out of the scarlet darkness, perfectly represents her vision of the society in which she is trapped, an uneasy and elfin dependent. "No jail was ever more secure," she tells us. And no jail, we soon learn, was ever more terrifying either, because this is the room where Mr. Reed, the only "father" Jane has ever had, "breathed his last." It is, in other words, a kind of patriarchal death chamber, and here Mrs. Reed still keeps "divers parchments, her jewel-casket, and a miniature of her dead husband" in a secret drawer in the wardrobe (chap. 2). Is the room haunted, the child wonders. At least, the narrator implies, it is realistically if not Gothically haunting, more so than any chamber in, say, *The Mysteries of Udolpho,* which established a standard for such apartments. For the spirit of a society in which Jane has no clear place sharpens the angles of the furniture, enlarges the shadows, strengthens the locks on the door. And the deathbed of a father who was not really her father emphasizes her isolation and vulnerability.

Panicky, she stares into a "great looking glass," where her own image floats toward her, alien and disturbing. "All looked colder and darker in that visionary hollow than in reality," the adult Jane explains. But a mirror, after all, is also a sort of chamber, a mysterious enclosure in which images of the self are trapped like "divers parchments." So the child Jane, though her older self accuses her of mere superstition, correctly recognizes that she is doubly imprisoned. Frustrated and angry, she meditates on the injustices of her life, and fantasizes "some strange expedient to achieve escape from insupportable oppression— as running away, or, if that could not be effected, never eating or drinking more, and letting myself die" (chap. 2). Escape through flight, or escape through starvation: the alternatives will recur throughout *Jane Eyre* and, indeed, ⟨. . .⟩ throughout much other nineteenth- and twentieth-century literature by women. In the red-room, however, little Jane chooses (or is chosen by) a third, even more terrifying, alternative: escape through madness. Seeing a ghostly, wandering light, as of the moon on the ceiling, she notices that "my heart beat thick, my head grew hot; a sound filled my ears, which I deemed the rushing of wings; something seemed near me; I was oppressed, suffocated: endurance broke down." The child screams and sobs in anguish, and then, adds the narrator coolly, "I suppose I had a species of fit," for her next memory is of waking in the nursery "and seeing before me a terrible red glare crossed with thick black bars" (chap. 3), merely the nursery fire of course, but to Jane Eyre the child a terrible reminder of the experience she has just had, and to Jane Eyre the adult narrator an even more dreadful omen of experiences to come.

For the little drama enacted on "that day" which opens *Jane Eyre* is in itself a paradigm of the larger drama that occupies the entire book: Jane's anomalous, orphaned position in society, her enclosure in stultifying roles and houses, and her attempts to escape through flight, starvation, and ⟨. . .⟩ madness. And that Charlotte Brontë quite consciously intended the incident of the red-room to serve as a paradigm for the larger plot of her novel is clear not only from its position in the narrative but also from Jane's own recollection of the experience at crucial moments throughout the book: when she is humiliated by Mr. Brocklehurst at Lowood, for instance, and on the night when she decides to leave Thornfield. In between these moments, moreover, Jane's pilgrimage consists of a series of experiences which are, in one way or another, variations on the central, red-room motif of enclosure and escape.

—Sandra M. Gilbert and Susan Gubar, "A Dialogue of Self and Soul: Plain Jane's Progress," *The Madwoman in the Attic: The Woman Writer and the Nineteenth-Century Literary Imagination* (New Haven: Yale University Press, 1979), pp. 339–41

JOHN MAYNARD ON SEXUALITY IN *JANE EYRE*

[John Maynard (b. 1941) is a professor of English at New York University and the author of *Browning's Youth* (1977) and *Charlotte Brontë and Sexuality* (1984), from which the following extract is taken. Here, Maynard finds the focus of *Jane Eyre* to be a portrayal of the obstacles in the way of mature sexual awakening.]

Jane's subsequent description of their ten years of life together continues the emphasis throughout the Ferndean scenes on their physical closeness. Jane feels supremely blest just because she is fully Rochester's life as he is hers: "No woman was ever nearer to her mate than I am: ever more absolutely bone of his bone, and flesh of his flesh." They have been knit especially closely by the early years of Rochester's dependence on her sight. Now they share heartbeats and conversation all day long. Few readers, even the most happily married in our divorcing age, will believe such a degree of exclusive mutual company, even between an engaging ex-governess and a man with a West Indian and European past, could be entirely satisfactory. This is a storybook ending, a paradise of satisfied love. The interesting point is that it is love conceived of as exceptionally physical, a meeting of bodies as well as true minds and hearts. Lest there be any question about the potency of this, Jane casually alludes to their first-born, leaving open how many children issued from their fruitful union.

Jane Eyre ends, somewhat unfortunately, with a very brief account of St John's missionary activity and his hope for the next world. If Brontë won't allow Jane, probably rightly in character, any irony over St John's disposal of all earthly joys, she nonetheless concludes the novel as a whole with a clear assertion of loving sexual union. Jane herself has manifestly been brought to a decisive choice between the alternatives of ascetic self-suppression and sexual fulfillment. Yet far more than *The Professor,* the work as a whole also speaks most clearly about the myriad obstacles, within and without the individual, to mature sexual awakening. Brontë uses lesser characters and symbolic structures to indicate the difficulties she sees in sexual openness. She shows how fears, conscious suppressions, and undeliberate repressions work within Jane's mind to drive her into anxiety and, finally, a panicked flight. She even builds into the plot of the book a series of obstacles that suggest her own anxieties: Rochester really is in some sense an illegal seducer; sex has helped drive Bertha mad; Rochester does pay a heavy price for his sins, however much this is qualified and ultimately requited. Because such fears of sexuality become actually incorporated into the world of the tale, they require balancing assertions of sexual growth within the plot, especially the timely elimination of Bertha and the marvelous call to Jane. The same nice balancing of forces of suppression and assertion is at work in the mythic world of the novel's action as in the finer analysis of Jane's psychological response or in the examination of sexual alternatives.

In all cases Brontë comes down finally on the side of sexual initiation—with caution. But the assertion on the side of the life force is far less valuable than the quality of the analysis. Brontë shows us on every level of the novel the complex interweaving strands in sexual life that make it at once so central to experience and so easily miswoven or unraveled. Jane's childhood, her early relations with those loving or unloving to her, her position in the world and her degree of independence, her relative inexperience, her moral and religious values, her sense of belonging to a family, her relation to supportive females or female images, her perception of the uses of sexual energies to different lovers, her need to sacrifice herself or others, all affect her capacity to undergo sexual awakening successfully. Brontë, unlike many of her critics, makes no simple case for how a complex individual functions. She lets Jane tell her tale, reveal her delicate and complicated responses, and challenge us to comprehend sexual experience in its complex totality. The result, for all its occasional naivetés, is one of the finest novels in English and a particularly splendid examination of the process of sexual awakening. Good as the studies of Caroline Vernon's seduction or Elizabeth Hastings's flight from sexuality were, this is miles further along. With tact and infinite delicacy Brontë unfolds and examines the sexual life. For this area of experience, so close to the unconscious world of symbolic language, she needs and finds language rarely drawn upon by as subtle a predecessor in psychological analysis as Jane Austen: strong symbols, dreams, mythic overlays, Gothic plot devices, descriptions of buildings or nature and the seasons. Yet the marvel is that in all this welter of large symbols and emotional signs there is the fundamental focus on the delicate workings of and adjustments to Jane's continuous inner life. She is no vague human counter moving through a turbulent world of symbols, though Lawrence's heroes and heroines sometimes are. Jane remains the center of human complexity around which Brontë's vision of the need for sexual fulfillment and its obstacles focus and concentrate. When we have read the work with the attention it deserves, we feel we have come perhaps as close as we shall in language to the infinitely subtle but not totally inexplicable process of sexual growth.

—John Maynard, *Charlotte Brontë and Sexuality* (Cambridge: Cambridge University Press, 1984), pp. 143–44

TOM WINNIFRITH ON THE AUTOBIOGRAPHICAL SIGNIFICANCE OF *JANE EYRE*

[Tom Winnifrith (b. 1938), senior lecturer in English and comparative literary studies at the University of Warwick in Coventry, England, has written prolifically on the Brontës. In this extract from *A New Life of*

Charlotte Brontë (1988), Winnifrith traces the features of *Jane Eyre* that appear to have been drawn from Brontë's own life.]

Charlotte's achievement in writing *Jane Eyre,* a brave novel about triumph against adversity, is a remarkable tribute to the resilience of the human heart, and though it is possible to find fault with Charlotte on various scores, nobody can doubt her indomitable courage. Her letters to Ellen Nussey in the winter of 1847, as well as complaining about the weather and about Branwell, describe the stifling boredom of her existence. 'I know life is passing away and I am doing nothing', 'I am now in that unenviable frame of mind—my humour I think is too soon overthrown—too sore—too demonstrative and vehement', 'I'm in danger sometimes of falling into self-weariness', 'I look almost old enough to be your mother—grey—sunk—and withered'.

From this dreary, middle-aged ennui Charlotte was able to create an exciting story with a happy ending about a young woman, who, in spite of cruel restricting disadvantages, wins her way to fulfilment and happiness by the strength of her character. There is, of course, something of Charlotte in Jane; the heroine's loneliness, sense of confinement and strong hatred of injustice are shared by the author. On the other hand certain scenes and characters and episodes in the plot appear to owe more to the fantastic world of Angria than to the drab world of Charlotte Brontë. It is these features of the novel which have received most criticism. The strange coincidences, the unreal atmosphere of the house party at Thornfield and the wild behaviour of Mr Rochester have seemed incredible to readers, both contemporary and modern.

Mr Rochester contains something of Monsieur Heger, something of Zamorna, but also ⟨. . .⟩ something of Charlotte herself, and he and his suitability for Jane are better appreciated in this light. Blanche Ingram and her entourage are artificial, but are of course meant to be; here Charlotte is using somewhat crude satire to take revenge on the world she felt had passed her by. The coincidences which recur in all the novels are perhaps harder to excuse. The way in which everybody in the novel seems to know everybody else is a consequence of Charlotte's restricted upbringing among a narrow circle of acquaintances. We would not really expect Miss Temple to know Mr Lloyd, the apothecary at Gateshead, or Mr Rochester to have much knowledge of Mr Brocklehurst. The fortunate device whereby Jane, alone and helpless, collapses outside the door of her long-lost cousins is as improbable as the similar scene in *Villette* where Lucy Snowe is rescued in a faint by her godmother's son. Both heroines are tempted to think that they may have found their husbands, and the other relationship, though clumsily established, does have something of the brother–sister link which is all that Jane wants from St John and Lucy can get from John Graham. It is probably wrong to make any equation between Diana and Mary Rivers, and Emily and Anne Brontë; the fictional heroines are outwardly more spirited and attractive, their relationship is not the same, and 〈. . .〉 there was probably rather less harmony at Haworth Parsonage than at Moor End.

The outrageous rescue by Rochester crying 'Jane' three times when she was about to accept the proposal of St John Rivers has offended many readers. It was apparently based on an incident in real life, but an exact identification is unlikely, and speculation about possible parallels fairly fruitless. It is of course necessary to have some strong reason for Jane to go back to Rochester, since if she had gone back on impulse without supernatural intervention she might well deserve St John's accusations of immorality.
> —Tom Winnifrith, *A New Life of Charlotte Brontë* (New York: St. Martin's Press, 1988), pp. 76–78

BETTINA L. KNAPP ON THE IMAGERY OF THE RED ROOM

[Bettina L. Knapp (b. 1926) is a professor at Hunter College and Graduate Center of the City University of New York and the author of *Liliane Atlan* (1988) and *The Brontës* (1991), from which the following extract is taken. Here, Knapp discusses the imagery of the red-room found at the beginning of *Jane Eyre*.]

The image of the *Red Room,* used symbolically by Charlotte at the outset of the novel, points up the psychologically injurious nature of Jane's early years, from infancy to the age of ten, spent in the home of her aunt, Mrs. Reed, who transfers her own frustrations—blending anger and venom—on the defenseless Jane. The most traumatic of the child's protracted punishments was confinement in the "red room," which she believed to be haunted. No warmth, understanding, or tenderness is received by Jane, who is also taunted and brutalized by Mrs. Reed's three spoiled children—particularly her son, John. Thrust on her own resources, the lonely waif lives the life of an exile. Here is an inward journey, perilous, tremulous, and painful.

That the red-room episode should have occurred at Gateshead, the name of Mrs. Reed's estate, is significant. Onomastically, Gateshead reinforces Jane's psychological condition of alienation and sense of imprisonment in a hopeless situation: a *gate* serves as a barrier preventing any free-flowing communication between the protagonist and the outside world; *head* implies Jane's psychological need to develop the thinking side of her personality while keeping her feeling world in check. She had to function analytically, through her *head* or *mind,* and keep her heart and emotions tightly sealed behing the *gate.*

Her restrictive ambiance not only activated bouts of despair in Jane, but also fired the volatile instinctual realm within her psyche. The hermetic sealing of one part of a person encourages an eventful flaring up of incarcerated forces. So powerful may these excoriating energetic charges become that they can no longer be contained, and ignite in sequences of uncontrollable episodes, with understandably devastating results.

To seek peace of mind, Jane would frequently sit in the window seat in the small breakfast room, drawing the *scarlet* drapery around her and thus shutting herself off from the Reed family. A sequence of metonymies—a cold winter scene with its "leafless shrubbery," its "raw twilight," its "storm-beat shrub," its "ceaseless rain sweeping away wildly before a long and lamentable blast"—reveals her condition of psychological deprivation. Within the relatively protected area, encircled symbolically by a fiery curtain, she was able not only to read her favorite books, but to gaze through the window towards freedom. After the fourteen-year-old John reprimands Jane, "a dependent" without money, for reading one of *his* books, he snatches it and flings it at Jane, who, in her attempt to avoid it, falls and strikes her head against the door. Cut and bleeding, she flashes out verbally: "Wicked and cruel boy! . . . murderer." John informs his mother of the incident and Jane is immediately locked up in the red room.

The "room," an enclosed area, is the locus of Jane's agon or struggle. Psychologically, her imprisonment in the red chamber may be viewed as a testing ground—an initiation—thus giving it ritualistic connotations. Functioning as a secret space, it is within this inner area that the heroine will begin to deal with her fears and learn to confront the vagaries of the life experience. Such a trial, undergone by so many heroines and heroes of past times, if successful, endows an initiate with the strength necessary to step into the next stage of development.

The color red, so horror provoking a hue for Jane, has ritualistic significance when identified with fire, warmth, and blood. Empirically speaking, red/blood is a life-giving and life-sustaining force. Because of Jane's highly religious orientation, red may be associated with the blood sacrifice of Christ in Holy Communion, which allows the initiate to bathe in transpersonal spheres. Red also stands for those earth-factors Jane represses: raw instinct, uncontrolled inner urges, and sexual passion.
—Bettina L. Knapp, *The Brontës* (New York: Continuum, 1991), pp. 144–46

ROBERT KENDRICK ON ROCHESTER'S CONVERSION

[Robert Kendrick is an American literary scholar who, in this extract, discusses Rochester's conversion to Christianity at the end of *Jane Eyre*. Kendrick finds that this conversion does not signal Rochester's return to patriarchal authority but rather a recognition of his own frailty.]

Though Rochester's conversion experience is what enables him to enter into a marriage with Jane in which he does not try to regain his lost patriarchal power, it would be a mistake to read this acceptance of God as a reaffirmation of a patriarchal discourse. As indicated earlier, Jane's faith appeals to a belief which runs "against the grain" of the Anglican structure, and though modern readers may be too quick to read the acceptance of religion in the novel as a capitulation to a dominant ideology, it should be remembered that for Jane, and for Rochester, belief becomes a means with which to create an oppositional self, not a means by which the self is "subjected" to the dominant social order. Peter Allan Dale notes that

> Rochester, his own conversion to Christianity notwithstanding, calls to her as 'the alpha and omega of his heart's wishes' (cf. Rev. 1:8), and she responds with her own resounding echo of Revelation: 'I am coming.' As the two are reunited, the language in which Jane describes their renewed relationship is really no less blasphemous than her earlier metaphorical association of their impending sexual union with the marriage of the Lamb.

Their eventual marriage takes them not only away from the order of landed society, but away from traditional religious conceptions of the husband as master. Though Rochester has certainly retained some patriarchal power—Jane notes that he dictates letters to her, correspondence that may represent business dealings, and indicates that she is not carrying on all of their relations, public or private—he is at the same time her dependent. His voiced acceptance of Divine justice amounts to an acceptance of a suspension of his own power, and a suspension of the decision of who exactly is to be the master in their marriage. This suspension of definite positions creates a just relation by virtue of the equitable sharing of domestic power between the two, and because their final identities will not come from intersubjective reflection, but from the divine decision that is yet to come, the "à-venir." Dale has noted that the speculative ending of the novel implies a partial rejection of "a particular historical structure of expectation," and though he is referring to narrative structure in this instance, it is not unrea-

sonable to conclude that this statement can refer to Brontë's relation to religious and "gendered" closure as well. The dominant imaginings of identity (of religion, class, gender, and the points at which these discourses intersect) no longer, in Dale's terms, "command implicit assent," but neither can they be escaped. The result is Brontë's subjection of the subject to a "higher" code which suspends all "subjection" by earthly discourses. This solution is provisional at best, but it is nonetheless an attempt to articulate an identity that cannot be contained by the dominant narratives.

Brontë creates her "ladies' man" in Edward Rochester by forcing her creation to envision himself not as the master but as an insufficient subject of God, thus revealing the ultimate powerlessness of patriarchal imaginings of male social and sexual power and making it necessary for him to imagine himself on terms which enable a just and ethical relationship between himself and Jane. Though the imperialist and racist biases of Brontë's text noted by Gayatri Spivak remain, there is at the same time a questioning of dominant imaginings of masculinity, and the social order which relies on these narratives for its self-legitimation.

—Robert Kendrick, "Edward Rochester and the Margins of Masculinity in *Jane Eyre* and *Wide Sargasso Sea*," *Papers on Language and Literature* 30, No. 3 (Summer 1994): 253–55

LYNDALL GORDON ON MEN AND WOMEN IN *JANE EYRE*

[Lyndall Gordon is the author of two biographies of T. S. Eliot, *Eliot's Early Years* (1977) and *Eliot's New Life* (1988), as well as biographies of Virginia Woolf (1984) and Charlotte Brontë (1995). In this extract from that work, Gordon discusses the personal conflicts of many of the male and female characters in *Jane Eyre*.]

Though Charlotte Brontë wrote at the onset of a long and still-advancing period when women must question the abuses of

power—sexual power, violence, militarism, and the evils these perpetuate—from an objective distance, men and women belong to the same species, sharing the same fundamental pattern of existence. Have we attractions as a species, we might well ask, and shall we go on? Jane, as survivor, with unflinching moral courage, reason in command of passion, and vigour which derives from vivacity of mind, embodies a principled resilience all can share. As orphan, she stands for all who are dependent and alone, who are vulnerable to abuse, both crass abuse of child, class, or woman, and also that more subtle abuse explored in all Charlotte Brontë's work: denial of feeling.

The bully, John Reed, cuffs Jane because she will not show him due deference. Brocklehurst humiliates Jane, and starves the girls at Lowood in order to break their spirit; but, when Jane looks back, it is his works—repressive, threatening, sanctimonious words—that remain the focus of resentment. What draws Jane to Rochester, despite his dubious past, his growls, and gloom, is that Rochester invites the opposite of this denial: 'I have not been petrified', Jane tells him when she explains her attachment. 'I have not been buried with inferior minds, and excluded from every glimpse of communion with what is bright, and energetic, and high.'

In contrast, Mr Brocklehurst and St John Rivers are pillars of a structure that denied the right of feeling to those it designed for service. The danger of this emotional imprisonment is the depletion of character, as Anne Brontë feared when she went 'flat' after her years with the Robinsons, or as Jane fears when Mr Rivers (saying 'I . . . I . . . I . . .'), insists on marriage to support his spiritual ambition.

Jane and Rochester both pass through their periods in the wilderness: Jane begging for food and shelter near Whitcross; Rochester a blind recluse at Ferndean, after the fire that destroys his house. Jane's self-reliance is tested under conditions of extremity when she is bereft of protection, money, the means for cleanliness, even the reserve dear to her pride. Rochester, in turn, is stripped of the sultan aspect of power— the power that had charmed the parasites (Céline, Giacinta, and Clara) of his licentious past. Sultan largesse had been an irritant to Jane: it would make her a ridiculous doll. Worse, it

had presumed to think for her, to plan a false wedding: '. . . I would not say he had betrayed me: but the attribute of stainless truth was gone from his idea; and from his presence I must go'. Yet all that is desirable in Rochester's power does survive this parting and their subsequent ordeals. Still retrievable beneath his encrustations of bitterness are his knowing, his verbal play, his ready engagement with Jane. The final chapter, which follows the pair through the first years of their marriage, asserts the success of sustained compatibility: 'We talk, I believe, all day long'.

This resolution of freedom and bonding comes about only when Jane has purged herself finally of two forms of tyranny. First, she must free herself of the tyranny of licence: the child's abandon to rage, and the adult's abandon to appetite that leads to the concealed frenzy in Rochester's home, Thornfield Hall.

Bertha Mason Rochester, the mad woman on the third floor, is a warning more than a character: a warning of mindless passion. Jane veers closest to her in one cancelled sentence in the manuscript which admits an underlying recklessness in her susceptibility to Rochester during their engagement: '. . . if he was subjugated so was I—and that by a strange and resistless sway'. This is checked after the disclosure of attempted bigamy, followed by the visit to Rochester's mad wife. Jane, alone in her room, stops the momentum of shared passion with the words (heavily underscored in the manuscript), 'but now—I thought.' Her reassertion of reason separates her sharply from the madness in which Rochester continues to remain implicated. Bertha embodies the anarchic element in Rochester, rampant until she is dead. Dying in her blaze of fire, she leaves him scarred and, to a degree, disabled. It is suggestive that it is Rochester she disables, not Jane. He has been scarred by his part in a long tradition of flawed judgement. For Bertha Mason never was a promising woman; she was thick, with slow, unmoving eyes, like those of her brother.

—Lyndall Gordon, *Charlotte Brontë: A Passionate Life* (New York: Norton, 1995), pp. 154–56

Works by Charlotte Brontë

Poems by Currer, Ellis, and Acton Bell (with Emily and Anne Brontë). 1846.

Jane Eyre: An Autobiography. 1848. 3 vols.

Shirley: A Tale. 1849. 3 vols.

Villette. 1853. 3 vols.

The Professor: A Tale. 1857. 2 vols.

The Adventures of Ernest Alembert: A Fairy Tale. Ed. Thomas J. Wise. 1896.

Poems by Charlotte, Emily, and Anne Brontë. 1902.

Richard Coeur de Lion and Blondel: A Poem. Ed. Clement K. Shorter. 1912.

Saul and Other Poems. 1913.

The Violet: A Poem Written at the Age of Fourteen. Ed. Clement K. Shorter. 1916.

Lament Befitting These "Times of Night." Ed. George E. MacLean. 1916.

The Red Cross Knight and Other Poems. 1917.

The Swiss Emigrant's Return and Other Poems. 1917.

The Orphans and Other Poems (with Emily and Branwell Brontë). 1917.

The Four Wishes: A Fairy Tale. Ed. Clement K. Shorter. 1918.

Latest Gleanings: Being a Series of Unpublished Poems from Her Early Manuscripts. Ed. Clement K. Shorter. 1918.

Napoleon and the Spectre: A Ghost Story. Ed. Clement K. Shorter. 1919.

Darius Codomannus: A Poem Written at the Age of Eighteen Years. 1920.

Complete Poems. Eds. Clement K. Shorter and C. W. Hatfield. 1923.

An Early Essay. Ed. M. H. Spielmann. 1924.

The Twelve Adventurers and Other Stories. Ed. Clement K. Shorter. 1925.

The Spell: An Extravaganza. Ed. George Edwin MacLean. 1931.

The Shakespeare Head Brontë (with Anne and Emily Brontë). Ed. Thomas J. Wise and John Alexander Symington. 1931–38. 19 vols.

Legends of Angria: Compiled from the Early Writings of Charlotte Brontë. Ed. Fanny E. Ratchford and William Clyde DeVane. 1933.

The Professor; Tales from Angria; Emma, a Fragment; Together with a Selection of Poems (with Emily and Anne Brontë). Ed. Phillis Bentley. 1954.

The Search after Happiness. Ed. T. A. J. Burnett. 1969.

Five Novelettes. Ed. Winifred Gérin. 1971.

The Novels of the Brontës (Clarendon Edition). Ed. Ian Jack et al. 1976– .

Two Tales. Ed. William Holtz. 1978.

Poems. Ed. Tom Winnifrith. 1984.

Poems: A New Text and Commentary. Ed. Victor A. Neufeldt. 1985.

The Juvenilia of Jane Austen and Charlotte Brontë. Ed. Frances Beer. 1986.

A Leaf from an Unopened Volume; or, The Manuscript of an Unfortunate Author: An Angria Story. Ed. Charles Lemon. 1985.

An Edition of the Early Writings of Charlotte Brontë. Ed. Christine Alexander. 1987.

Works about Charlotte Brontë and Jane Eyre

Alexander, Christine. *The Early Writings of Charlotte Brontë*. Oxford: Blackwell, 1983.

Allott, Miriam, ed. *Charlotte Brontë: Jane Eyre and Villette: A Casebook*. London: Macmillan, 1973.

Barker, Judith R. V. *The Brontës*. London: Weidenfeld & Nicolson, 1994.

Beer, Patricia. *Reader, I Married Him: A Study of the Women Characters of Jane Austen, Charlotte Brontë, Elizabeth Gaskell, and George Eliot*. New York: Harper & Row, 1974.

Berg, Maggie. *Jane Eyre: Portrait of a Life*. Boston: Twayne, 1987.

Bloom, Harold, ed. *The Brontës*. New York: Chelsea House, 1987.

————, ed. *Charlotte Brontë's Jane Eyre*. New York: Chelsea House, 1987.

Bock, Carol. *Charlotte Brontë and the Storyteller's Audience*. Iowa City: University of Iowa Press, 1992.

Burkhart, Charles. *Charlotte Brontë: A Psychosexual Study of Her Novels*. London: Gollancz, 1973.

Chase, Karen. *Eros and Psyche: The Representation of Personality in Charlotte Brontë, Charles Dickens, and George Eliot*. New York: Methuen, 1984.

Duthie, Enid Lowry. *The Brontës and Nature*. New York: St. Martin's Press, 1986.

Ewbank, Inga-Stina. *Their Proper Sphere: A Study of the Brontë Sisters as Early-Victorian Female Novelists*. Cambridge, MA: Harvard University Press, 1966.

Fraser, Rebecca. *The Brontës: Charlotte Brontë and Her Family*. New York: Crown, 1988.

Gaskell, Elizabeth. *The Life of Charlotte Brontë.* 1857. Ed. Alan Shelston. Harmondsworth: Penguin, 1975.

Gérin, Winifred. *Charlotte Brontë: The Evolution of Genius.* New York: Oxford University Press, 1967.

Gezari, Janet. *Charlotte Brontë and Defensive Conduct: The Author and the Body at Risk.* Philadelphia: University of Pennsylvania Press, 1992.

Gordon, Felicia. *A Preface to the Brontës.* London: Longman, 1989.

Imlay, Elizabeth. *Charlotte Brontë and the Mysteries of Love: Myth and Allegory in* Jane Eyre. Brighton, UK: Harvester Wheatsheaf, 1989.

Keefe, Robert. *Charlotte Brontë's World of Death.* Austin: University of Texas Press, 1979.

Kucich, John. *Repression in Victorian Fiction: Charlotte Brontë, George Eliot, and Charles Dickens.* Berkeley: University of California Press, 1988.

Linder, Cynthia. *Romantic Imagery in the Novels of Charlotte Brontë.* New York: Barnes & Noble, 1978.

Macpherson, Pat. *Reflecting on* Jane Eyre. London: Routledge, 1989.

Mitchell, Judith. *The Stone and the Scorpion: The Female Subject of Desire in the Novels of Charlotte Brontë, George Eliot, and Thomas Hardy.* Westport, CT: Greenwood Press, 1994.

Moglen, Helene. *Charlotte Brontë: The Self Conceived.* New York: Norton, 1976.

Nestor, Pauline. *Female Friendships and Communities: Charlotte Brontë, George Eliot, Elizabeth Gaskell.* Oxford: Clarendon Press, 1985.

Parkin-Gounelas, Ruth. *Fictions of the Female Self: Charlotte Brontë, Olive Schreiner, Katherine Mansfield.* London: Macmillan, 1991.

Peters, Margot. *Charlotte Brontë: Style in the Novel.* Madison: University of Wisconsin Press, 1973.

Prentis, Barbara. *The Brontë Sisters and George Eliot: A Unity of Difference.* Basingstoke, UK: Macmillan Press, 1988.

Schacht, Paul. "*Jane Eyre* and the History of Self-Respect." *Modern Language Quarterly* 52 (1991): 423–53.

Showalter, Elaine. *A Literature of Their Own: British Women Novelists from Brontë to Lessing.* Princeton: Princeton University Press, 1977.

Sutherland, Kathryn. "*Jane Eyre*'s Literary History: The Case for *Mansfield Park.*" *ELH* 59 (1992): 409–40.

Tayler, Irene. *Holy Ghosts: The Male Muses of Emily and Charlotte Brontë.* New York: Columbia University Press, 1990.

Wheat, Patricia H. *The Adytum of the Heart: The Literary Criticism of Charlotte Brontë.* Rutherford, NJ: Fairleigh Dickinson University Press, 1992.

Williams, Judith. *Perception and Expression in the Novels of Charlotte Brontë.* Ann Arbor, MI: UMI Research Press, 1988.

Winnifrith, Tom. *The Brontës.* London: Macmillan, 1977.

———. *The Brontës and Their Background: Romance and Reality.* New York: Barnes & Noble, 1973.

———. *Charlotte and Emily Brontë: Literary Lives.* Basingstoke, UK: Macmillan Press, 1989.

Young, Arlene. "The Monster Within: The Alien Self in *Jane Eyre* and *Frankenstein.*" *Studies in the Novel* 23 (1991): 325–38.

Zare, Bonnie. "*Jane Eyre*'s Excruciating Ending." *CLA Journal* 37 (1993): 204–20.

Zonana, Joyce. "The Sultan and the Slave: Feminist Orientalism and the Structures of *Jane Eyre.*" *Signs* 18 (1992–93): 592–617.

Index of
Themes and Ideas